PAPUA NEW GUINEA

Social Science

Grade 6

Stephen Ranck

OXFORD

Level 8, 737 Bourke Street, Docklands, Victoria 3008, Australia

Oxford University Press is a department of the University of Oxford. It furthers the University's objective of excellence in research, scholarship, and education by publishing worldwide in

Oxford New York

Auckland Cape Town Dar es Salaam Hong Kong Karachi Kuala Lumpur Madrid Melbourne Mexico City Nairobi New Delhi Shanghai Taipei Toronto

With offices in

Argentina Austria Brazil Chile Czech Republic France Greece Guatemala Hungary Italy Japan Poland Portugal Singapore South Korea Switzerland Thailand Turkey Ukraine Vietnam

OXFORD is a trademark of Oxford University Press in the UK and in certain other countries

First published 2006
Reprinted 2006, 2007, 2008, 2009 (twice), 2010, 2013, 2014, 2015, 2017, 2018, 2021, 2022, 2024, 2025

ISBN 978 0 19 555277 5

Typeset by Damage Design, Victoria, Australia
Printed in Singapore by Markono Print Media Pte Ltd

Contents

Introduction

WHAT IS SOCIAL SCIENCE?

Social science studies people. Social science looks at how people think and what people do. It studies people in groups and communities. Social science can also study people and their environment.

How do people interact with the environment around them?

The land is part of the environment. The land provides many resources.

In picture 1 the land is being used by local people to provide food.
In picture 2 tourists come to look at landscapes and attend tourist activities. This provides some income for the local people.

How do people organise themselves in groups?

In picture 1 on page ii, this group of students has a teacher who is being paid by the government. The students' parents must also pay school fees. Both girls and boys are learning.
In picture 2 no one is being paid to teach the children. It is a very different type of learning.
We begin to see that there are many different ways to study people. Because of this, there are many different types of social science. For example,

- Some parts of social science study people, the environment and how people use its resources.
- Other parts of social science explore societies and culture. They look at how people behave, at their attitudes and how people act in different groups.

Science and social science

Social science is part of science.

- Scientists start with looking at what is happening in their area of interest.
- This leads to an idea or a question for which they give a possible answer.
- They gather information about it.
- They observe and see if the information supports their answer.
- A conclusion is made that will either support or reject the scientist's answer. Sometimes, the results are not sufficient and more information is required.
- The conclusion should help to predict what will happen next time this question is asked.

Social science follows this same process, but social scientists study people and how they interact with each other, with other communities and with their environment.

For you to try

- In a group, discuss how you could study groups of people shown on the previous page.
- What information would you seek? Why ?
- How would you use this information as a social scientist to assist the groups shown?

Environment and Resources

Chapter summary

In this chapter you will have an opportunity to:

- ✓ identify and investigate the physical and natural environment
- ✓ identify and investigate the major features of the natural environment
- ✓ identify and investigate the major features of the human environment
- ✓ learn how to adapt to, change and sustain the physical environment.

Syllabus references

Strand: Environment and Resources

Substrand: People and Environment

Outcomes

Students are able to:

6.1.1 identify and describe local human-made and natural environments

6.1.2 identify the effects of the local natural environment on people

6.1.3 examine and describe people's impact on the local physical environment and take appropriate action

6.1.4 identify, propose and practice sustainable use of the local environment

6.1.5 identify the signs, causes and effects of local hazardous natural events and ways of responding to them

The Physical and Human Environment

THE PHYSICAL (NATURAL) ENVIRONMENT

There are six major features in the natural environment.

1. Climate

This is the pattern of temperature, rainfall, sunshine and wind in an area.

2. Landforms

This is how the land is shaped around you. There are many types of landforms like mountains, beaches and plains.

3. Geology

This is what occurs under the ground. Road cuttings are a good place to see your local geology.

4. Animals

This includes all the living creatures found in the environment.

5. Vegetation

This includes all the plants found in the environment. There might be kunai grass, forests, or swamp plants like sago palms.

6. Soil

This is the ground. Soil is the thin surface layer that covers the Earth's crust. It might be sand, loam or volcanic material.

For you to try

- Investigate your own community. What examples of these features can you find in the natural environment? Write them down and compare your list with your class.
- Design a poster that summarises all the features of your local environment.

How do these natural features influence each other?

Example: Port Moresby

In Port Moresby, the climate includes a long dry season. This limits plant growth and there are poor soils in many places. The result is grassland in some parts of the environment.

Look again at the above diagram. Where does the soil come from?

- Soil starts to form when the rock beneath the ground breaks up. This is caused by water and chemicals.
- Climate provides the water and the heat.

So we can say that soils are influenced by climate, and by geology which provides the rock.

Animals also influence soils.

- Ants, worms and other creatures live in the soil. They burrow through it, turn it over and expose it to the air. They also add droppings to the soil and create chemicals that change the soil.
- Larger animals like pigs root up the soil and add their droppings to it.
- Many animals become part of the soil when they die.

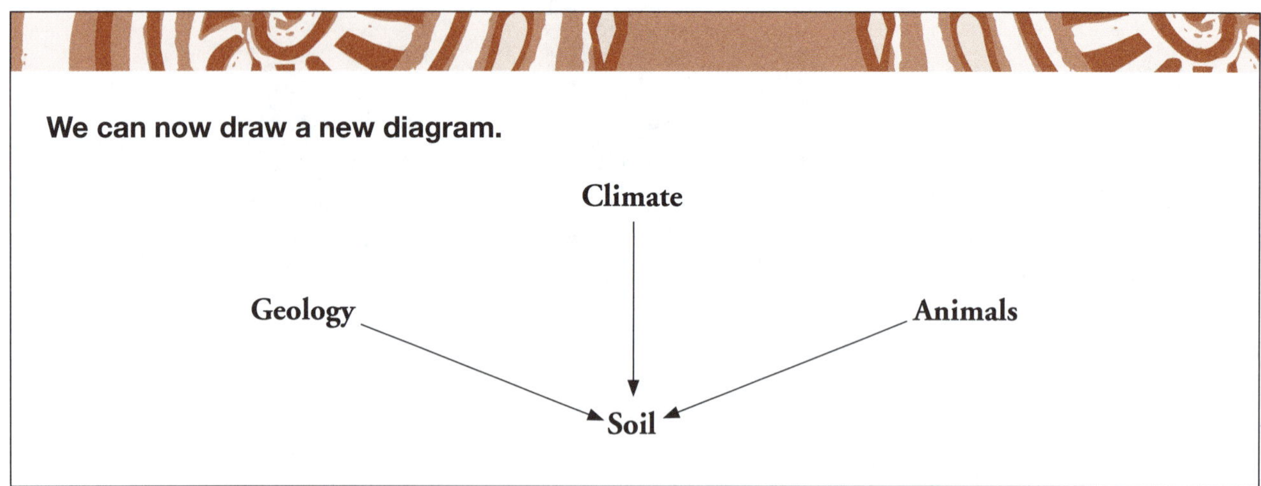

We have said that soil has an influence on vegetation. But vegetation has an influence on soil too. For example, look at the soil beneath the grass and compare it with the soil beneath the forest.

- Tree roots usually go much deeper than grass roots.
- The roots help break up the rock and help to make more soil.
- Trees also produce much more dead and rotting vegetation. This mixes with the soil and can provide food for some of the animals in the soil.

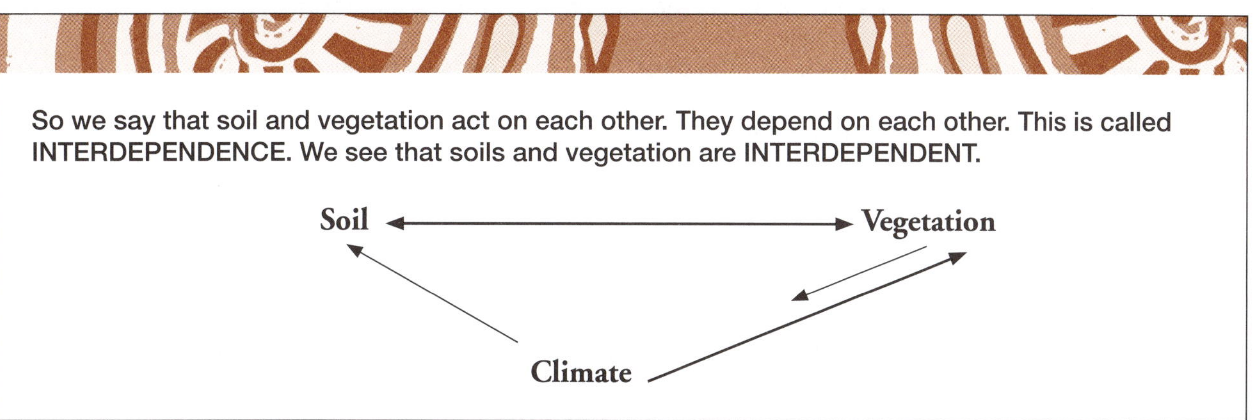

So we say that soil and vegetation act on each other. They depend on each other. This is called INTERDEPENDENCE. We see that soils and vegetation are INTERDEPENDENT.

Some parts of the environment can be stronger forces than others. For example, the diagram shows that the impact of climate on vegetation is much stronger than the impact of vegetation on climate.

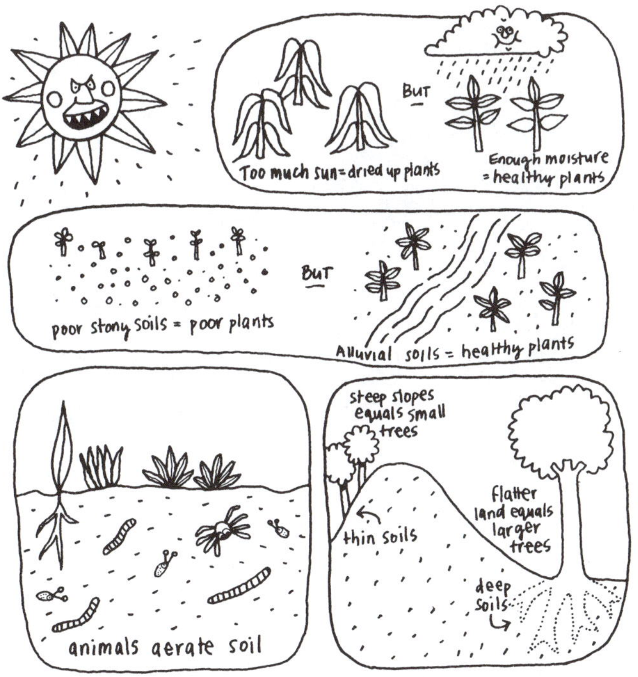

No matter how strong or how small, all parts of the environment influence each other.

This means they are interdependent. If you change one part of the environment, sooner or later other parts will change.

Interdependence—Sepik

Here is a good example of interdependence among animals, vegetation and soil.

The flying fox is called the 'little gardener' in parts of the Sepik. This is because the flying fox eats fruit from the trees and then spreads the seeds across the forest in its droppings.

The flying fox needs the fruit to eat and the trees need the seeds to be spread.

New trees then help protect and deepen the soil.

Village Sepik people understand this. They really like the flying fox spreading betelnut.

For you to try

- Can you find an example of interdependence in your local area?
- Ask your parents and other older people for examples.
- Present your findings as a report to the class.
- Draw pictures or make diagrams of the your best examples for display

Landforms

Landforms are major natural features of the land. The largest landforms are continents and oceans. The common landforms of Papua New Guinea include:

- Mountains and hills
- Islands
- Plains
- Valleys
- Rivers and swamps
- Catchments and watersheds
- Combination of landforms.

1. Mountains and hills

Older mountains are more rounded and gentle than younger mountains which are very steep. Papua New Guinea has younger mountains. They are very steep. Water rushes out of them today carving V-shaped valleys. Hills are smaller than mountains. The definition of what is a hill and what is a mountain varies between places. Mountains are much higher than hills.

2. Islands

Papua New Guinea is the second largest island in the world. Only Greenland is bigger. There are many types of islands in Papua New Guinea.

Some islands are formed due to volcano activity. Kar Kar is a volcanic island.

Some islands have been made through deposition, (adding material). Daru is a good example.

Some islands have been made by rising sea levels that flood lowlands and leave the peaks of mountains and hills surrounded by the sea. Islands in Milne Bay are a good example.

Some islands are made of coral. There are many types of coral reefs and coral islands. One special type of coral reef is the atoll. Atolls are a special type of island with coral growing in a big circle.

3. Plains

Plains are smooth and flat, sometimes with gently rolling small hills. There are coastal plains in many parts of Papua New Guinea and in parts of the Sepik.

4. Valleys

Valleys can be formed in many different ways. The most common way in Papua New Guinea is through the action of water.

Running water results in V-shaped valleys.

Frozen water can create glaciers. These are frozen rivers of ice which slowly move and carry material to grind out U-shaped valleys. There are U-shaped valleys in the Highlands that were created by glaciers in the past.

5. Rivers

Rivers are a very important part of the environment in Papua New Guinea. A river is a large natural watercourse. Smaller rivers that feed into a big river are called tributaries.

Rivers carry water and suspended materials to flood plains, swamps and the sea. The materials carried in the water are called sediments. These sediments help build soils and feed wetlands.

Many rivers in the world are polluted by human activities. People add chemicals, excessive earth, human waste and solid waste (rubbish) to the rivers. Protecting rivers is part of protecting catchments and a watershed.

6. Catchments and watersheds

A catchment is the total area of land covered by water, like a river or lake. Water starts as rain landing in the catchment. The water will flow in small streams into the rivers and then into a final large river that then empties into the sea.

Example: The Purari delta is the end of the Purari catchment.

Water can also flow to underground water reserves in a catchment area.

Watersheds are much larger than catchments. Watersheds often start with a mountain ridge. The watershed is all the rain that falls on one side of a mountain range and flows in one general direction into many rivers. It includes the water below the ground too, like catchments.

NOTE: Human activity anywhere in a watershed or catchment can cause problems with the water.

7. Combination of landforms

Different landforms may be found mixed together. You may find hills rising out of parts of a plain, or plateaus, mountains and hills close together. Papua New Guinea can be divided into regions where different sorts of landforms are common. These regions include:

- Southern plains and lowlands that are mainly plains with hills
- Central ranges that are mainly mountains with some basins and plateaus
- Sepik-Ramu that is mainly plains
- Northern ranges has a mixture of all types of landforms
- Islands also have a mixture of all types of landforms.

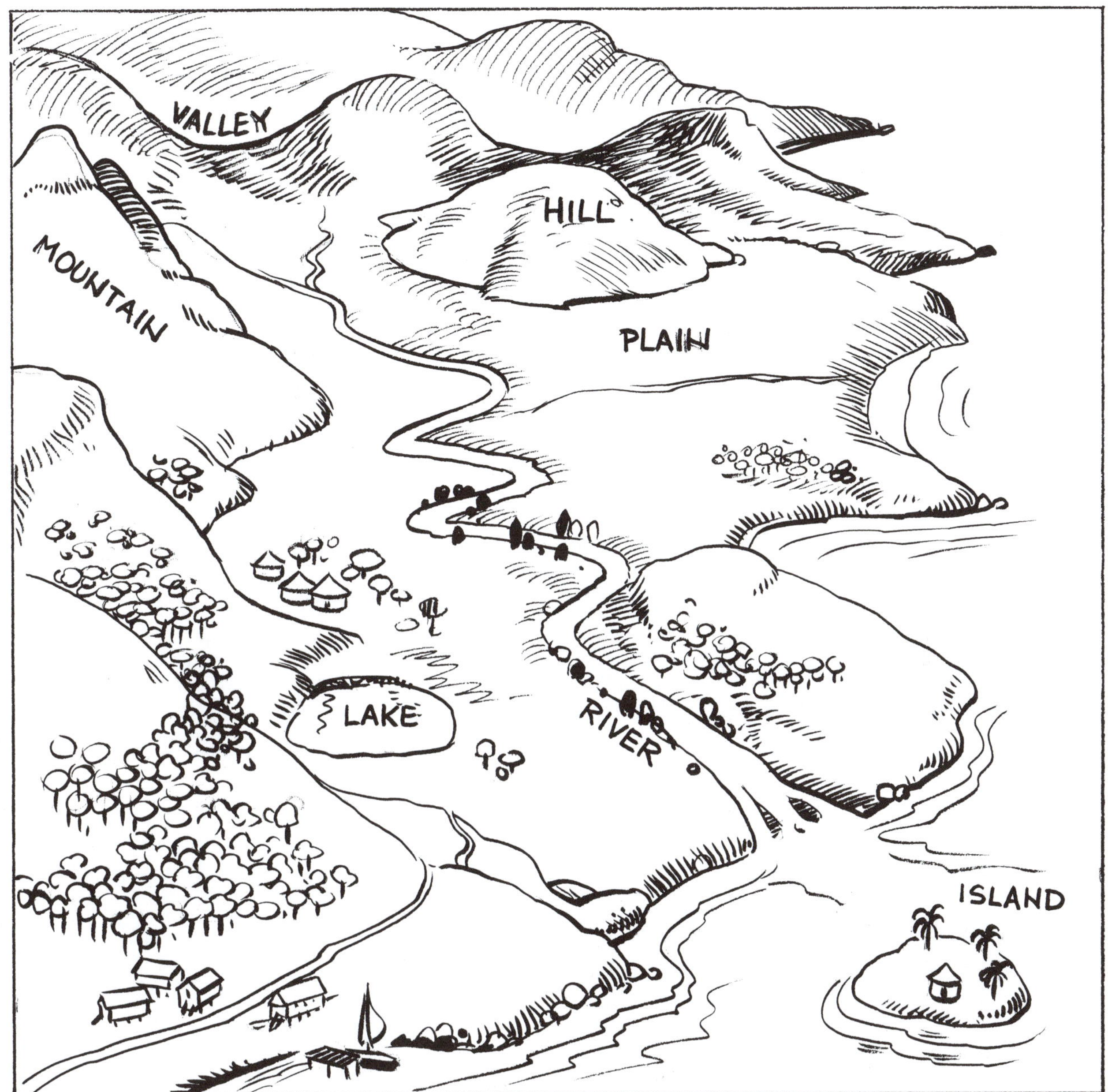

For you to try

- Describe the landforms found in your local area.
- Discuss ways that these landforms affect other parts of your environment.
- Explore your environment. Can you find examples of natural landforms and of landforms that have been influenced by human activities?

Vegetation

Vegetation can be described as all the plants that grow in a particular area. Over time, plants slowly change to make the best use of their environment, but they are easily destroyed by the activities of people. Vegetation is important to the environment because:

- roots of plants prevent erosion of soil.
- the leaves of plants allow the water to escape back to the air.
- plants use up carbon dioxide and change it to oxygen. We must have oxygen to breathe.
- plants provide nearly all our food.

Papua New Guinea has many different types of vegetation. Different plants are found in different places in Papua New Guinea. Vegetation types include:

Mangrove swamp

- Mangroves only grow in salty water, usually between the levels of the tide
- Many types of fish and other sea life live in mangrove swamps. Damage or destruction of mangroves destroys places for fish, prawns and crabs to reproduce.

Swamp

- Found in wet areas not affected by the sea
- Wet because of climate or nearby rivers on flat land
- Sometimes include trees and palms, but mostly very tall grass.

Savannah

- A mixture of scattered trees, grasses and ferns
- There are dry savannahs and wetland savannahs.

Lowland forest

- Very tall trees with much undergrowth
- Many different sorts of trees and plants and creepers
- Usually in areas of high rainfall
- Supports many animals, birds and insects
- Rich in timber, incuding kwila, rosewood, taun and ebony.

Mountain forest

- Found above 1000 metres where the temperature is lower and the forest is covered in mist and cloud most of the time
- Moss and running bamboo are common
- Home to many rare and endangered species
- Trees are often shorter and thinner than those in the lowlands.

Lowland grasslands

- Generally found in drier areas
- Often subject to frequent fires.

Mountain grasslansds

- Above 2500 metres
- Mainly grasses and shrubs
- Trees are usually small and few in number
- Frost is common.

For you to try

- Can you identify the different types of natural vegetation of your area?
- Discuss in class how it interacts with other parts of the environment.
- Does it provide a special home for some types of animals?
- If you are in a mountain area, can you find changes in the vegetation and temperatures as you go higher up the mountains?
- Do people have different names for the different vegetation systems?

Climate and weather

Weather

Weather is used to describe each day in terms of sun, cloud, rain, wind, humidity and heat.

- Rain is measured in millimetres.
- Wind is measured in kilometres per hour.
- Humidity is the amount of moisture in the air.
- Temperature is measured in degrees Celsius.

The weather changes every day. One day may be sunny and hot; the next day may be wet and cool. The weather can change in less than an hour in the mountains. People must be careful and prepared. Often it is sunny and warm in the morning in Goroka, but rainy and cool in the afternoon. People have died in the higher mountains because they have not been prepared for sudden changes in the weather.

Climate

Climate is the pattern of the weather over many years. Papua New Guinea has a tropical climate—generally it is hot and wet for the whole year. However, if we look at the climate figures for different places, we can see that the climate varies from place to place.

- The climate for the Highlands tends to be warm and mild with rain throughout the year.
- Coastal Papua New Guinea tends to be more seasonal with wet and drier periods.

The map below shows the climate regions of our nation.

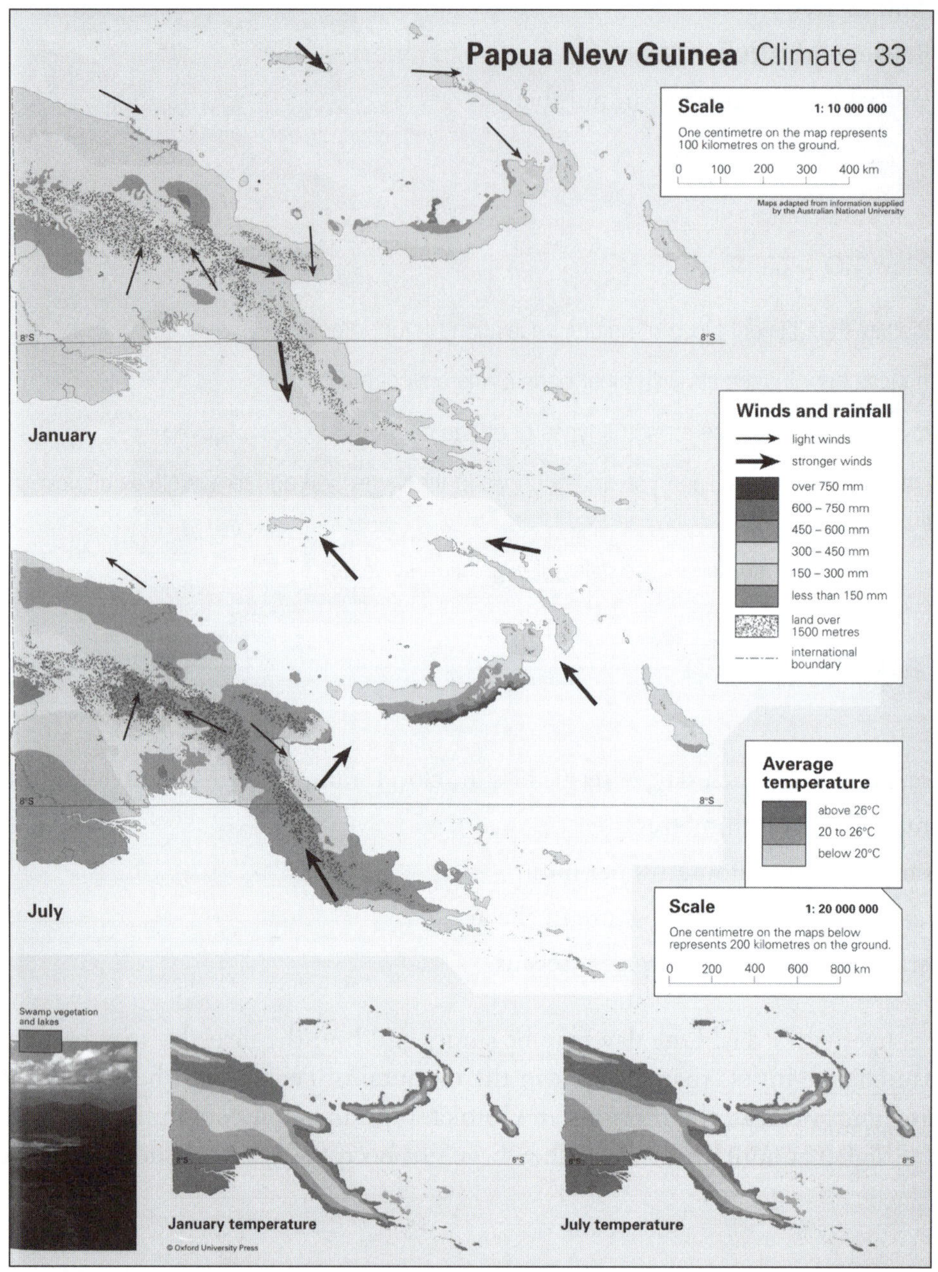

For you to try

- Find weather reports in copies of the newspaper.
- Compare the weather in your community with the weather in other communities. Do the different types of weather indicate different types of climates?
- Discuss the type of climate that you live in.

THE HUMAN ENVIRONMENT

People choose to live where they can best satisfy their needs for shelter, food and water. This depends on the resources of the environment they live in.

The human environment covers two areas—urban and rural. Most Papua New Guinea people live in rural areas. Only 20% of people live in urban areas. This means that for every 100 people in PNG, 80 are rural dwellers and 20 are urban dwellers.

The urban environment

- The urban environment is made up of towns and cities.
- Cities are bigger than towns and have different parts to them. These are often called zones or districts.
- The heart of the city is the central business district.
- There are residential districts where people live.
- There are commercial, industrial and administrative districts or zones where people work.
- Buildings, houses, roads, and special places like airports take up much of a city or town's space. They are parts of the built environment. They are created by humans.

The urban environment can also impact on the rural environment as cities need many resources from the countryside. For example, dams may be built on rivers in rural areas. These dams collect water and produce electricity for people in the city. The lake that forms behind the dam changes the surrounding local environment. The dam changes the river environment too.

The rural environment and rural settlements

- The rural environment includes forests, mountains, villages and most of the coast.
- Agriculture is very important to the rural environment.
- People still use parts of the rural environment for hunting and gathering.
- Most rural people live in villages. Villages in different parts of the country have different ways of life.
- There are many types of village settlements. Settlements are based on where people put their houses. The local environment helps to make what a village looks like.

Village settlements

- Some are clusters of houses. Some people will have two houses, one in the village and a smaller field house for tending crops.
- Another type of settlement is ribbon settlement that strings along a road, mountain ridge or coastline.
- A third type is scattered housing where people may live close to their crops.

Agriculture

There are three major types of agriculture:

1. Growing food for home use—feeding extra amounts to livestock or selling it in local markets
2. Smallholder cash crops like coffee, copra, cocoa, vanilla and betel nut
3. Plantation cash crops like coffee, copra, cocoa, palm oil, rubber and sugar.

For you to try

- Study each picture. Discuss the patterns these activities make on the rural environment. Can you find them around your community or are the patterns different?

Shifting cultivation

Shifting cultivation is often called slash-and-burn agriculture. It has been used in some places for thousands of years. Small plots of forest are burned. This removes weeds and the ash fertilises the soil. Burning also destroys some parts of the soil.

As the forest grows back the soil is restored. It can take up to 30 years, however, before the forest is ready for cropping again.

Many rural people understand the slash-and-burn system of agriculture. They know that there are stages of regrowth. The stages are called succession. Each stage can support different types and numbers of animals. People know that the last stage has the 'good' trees that tell them the soil is ready again for planting. If people start burning at an earlier stage, the danger is that the seed for later stages will be lost.

The biggest problem occurs when there are too many people and not enough forest. The result can be grassland, less food and more land disputes.

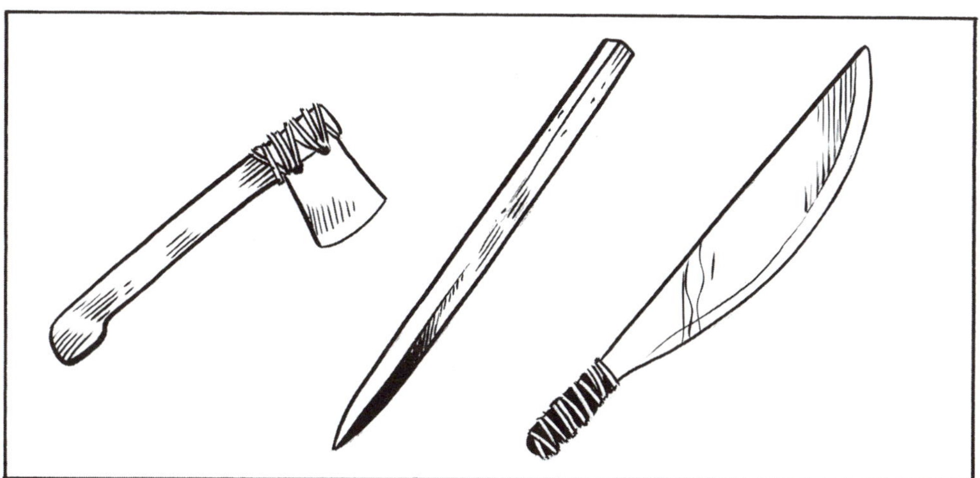

Shifting cultivation uses simple tools.

Plantation agriculture

Plantation agriculture often concentrates workers in a camp. It may also use seasonal labour. In Papua New Guinea, plantations grow copra, cocoa, coffee, rubber and tea. Plantation agriculture has many costs, such as heavy use of pesticides and herbicides. This may impact on the environment.

Smallholders are usually subsistence farmers who also grow cash crops in order to make money. Many smallholders living around a plantation grow the same crop as the plantation and sell their crop to the plantation.

For you to try

- Study each picture. Discuss the patterns these activities make on the rural environment. Can you find them around your community or are the patterns different?

Mining and forestry

Mining and forestry can also affect the rural environment. Sometimes they will create towns.

Mining and forestry can damage water catchments and watersheds. They can add poisons and earth materials to rivers. This can damage or destroy drinking water, fishing and other river life. Sometimes they can totally change rivers.

Papua New Guinea's land and its soil are very valuable natural resources. They are in danger and must be managed carefully. The resources available for hunting, fishing and gathering are decreasing. The population is increasing. More land is needed to grow food. Food crops and cash crops are competing for the best land. Already in some parts of the country, the best land is being used for growing cash crops. Food production is being pushed to less fertile land. Throughout this whole process people are changing the natural environment.

THE EFFECTS OF THE LOCAL PHYSICAL ENVIRONMENT ON PEOPLE

Adapting to the environment

Everywhere that people live, they make changes in the way they live to adapt to the environment.

To adapt means to change or adjust your situation. You can adapt to a rainy day by using an umbrella or a large leaf to protect you from the rain. If it is a very hot and sunny day, you can adapt to the heat by staying in the shade. Then you can cool off and play in the late afternoon rain.

Let's look at how people in Papua New Guinea have adapted to their environments.

Diet

Many diets use what grows best in the natural environment, for example sago. People discovered how to process sago, and sago now forms an important part of their diet. Rural people in coastal areas such as Manus smoke it with coconut to make a tasty dish that can be preserved for months.

Malaria

The malaria parasite is carried by anopheles mosquitos. In traditional times many Papua New Guineans adapted to malaria by building an immunity or resistance. This is now more difficult because many different strains of malaria are being carried quickly around the country.

People adapted by:

- leaving malaria areas
- sleeping under mosquito nets, particularly treated nets.

Housing

In many parts of Papua New Guinea people have adapted to the wet climate by building their houses on stilts. Transportation is by canoes and boats rather than road.

People have adapted to the tropical climate by building meeting houses that are open and airy for comfort, but protected from rain and hot sun.

People in the Highlands have adapted to a cooler climate by having houses with thicker walls and roofs located on the ground. This design keeps warm air inside and cold air outside.

How people on the Sepik River adapt to their environment

People have had to adapt to the rise and fall of the Sepik River because it rises about 3 to 5 metres each year. In the high water time, the river flows through some parts of the villages and people move about in canoes.

The Sepik house is especially adapted for a hot and wet environment.

- It is on stilts to prevent flooding.
- The very high roof allows hot air to rise and cooler air to stay below.
- The cool air moves under the house and keeps people cooler.

High water in the river is a time of plenty.

- The raised river brings resources the river such as large trees and the animals that live in those trees.
- Resources from far away, like sago and fishing and hunting areas, can be reached in canoes which are fast and can carry more resources. When it is low water, it is a long hard walk.

The way people plant on the riverbank is another adaptation.

- River flooding brings rich soil to the riverbanks. It is called alluvial soil and crops grow well in this soil.
- Planting is done on the rise and fall of the river. People plant in this soil when the river falls and harvest just before the river rises.
- People have to plant crops such as special yam varieties which can mature in six months. If the crops cannot be harvested in six months they will drown as the river waters rise.

For you to try

- Go on an excursion around your community to look at traditional housing. What housing styles have people used to adapt to the environment? What local tree and plant materials were used?
- Draw a traditional house and label the features that were designed to adapt to the local environment. (You can draw on paper or you can make a model.)
- Identify the nearest large natural feature close to your community. It could be the coast, a river, swamp or forest. Invite a government officer to talk about how have people adapted to using this natural environment. Write a short report and illustrate it with diagrams or drawings.
- Discuss how your local community has adapted to the physical environment. In your discussion , consider conditions such as average temperatures, soil quality, landforms, closeness to the sea, animals and vegetation.
- If your community has a pattern of wet and dry seasons, explain how activities change to adapt to this type of climate. What is done during the wet time? What happens when it is dry? How do activities change?

PEOPLE'S IMPACT ON THE LOCAL PHYSICAL ENVIRONMENT

It takes time for people to learn how to adapt to the environment. Often it is much quicker to change the environment. People are constantly changing their environment.

Urban environment

Cities are a good example of people changing their environment.

Let's look at an office building in the city. To build office buildings:

- soil is scraped away
- foundations are placed in the bedrock below
- vegetation is removed and concrete and asphalt covers much of the remaining soil
- most animals disappear because their habitat is destroyed.

The impact of cities on the natural environment can cause many problems.

Water

A city needs large quantities of water for household and industrial uses. To solve this problem dams are built which means land is lost. Cities produce waste water that can pollute downstream water resources.

Waste

Cities produce large amounts of solid waste. Solid waste is another name for rubbish. It can be burned up, buried or put in the sea. All these methods have problems.

- Burning at low temperatures pollutes the air.
- Burying rubbish can contaminate underground water.
- Dumping in the sea pollutes the sea and can add poisons that harm sea life.

Some solid waste can be recycled.

Good sanitation is needed to stop the spread of disease. Human waste needs to be specially treated. Cholera and diarrhoea are diseases that can come from poor sanitation.

Air pollution

Urban air pollution is:

- exhaust from motor vehicles
- smoke and other gases from factories
- other smoke that goes into the air from cities.

This damages the air quality. It can hurt people's lungs and create other health problems.

Vegetation and introduced species

The city removes and changes much of the vegetation. There is no place left for many of the animals that used to live there. Introduced species like the Norwegian rat have moved into most cities of the world. Other introduced species to PNG cities (and rural areas) that cause problems are cane toads, African snails, and the mimosa tree.

The city environment can make living more comfortable in many ways.

- **Roads and footpaths make transportation easier.**
- **There are many services for people offered by business and government such as health, education, entertainment, shopping and communications. This is possible because cities have many people in a small area. Service costs can be lower than for rural areas.**

For you to try

- Go on an excursion to a town or city near your school. Walk around the town and observe community services as well as community problems. Present this information in a table. How do you think community services could be improved and problems solved?

Rural environment

People in rural areas also make changes to the environment.

Land cultivation

Some forest areas in Papua New Guinea became savannah or grassland. This happened because fire was used many times for agriculture and hunting. The problem was that the time between crops was not long enough. The use of the slash-and-burn method changed the Highlands from forests to grasslands.

As the population grows in rural areas, more land is used and even less time is allowed for the soil to recover from cropping. More people are trying to grow crops using a system that can damage soils.

Land is also cleared in places where it is too wet to use fire. People cut away plants to free space for crops. They know that if they cut everything the rain will wash the soil away. So they leave big trees to protect the soil. Parts of Southern Highlands, Gulf and Western provinces are good examples of this. Bad farming or gardening can cause erosion. This is when the soil is washed away.

Pesticides and fertilisers

There are others costs or damage to the environment. Pesticides and fertilisers are used on crops but can wash away into rivers and the sea. They can damage the fish and other life in the water and make the water unsafe to drink. Pesticides and fertilisers can also harm the wildlife on the land.

Animals

Raising animals also changes the environment. Land is cleared so food can be grown for the animals. Some animals escape and change the environment. Pigs and dogs escaped long ago to become wild pigs and wild dogs. Crops can also escape. For example, bird's eye chillies are a cash crop that is now found growing wild in many parts of the country.

When people change the environment it has good and bad results.

Good results

- People have more food and a more comfortable life.
- The land is more productive and meets the needs of the people.
- Gardens produce food for villages.
- The growing of cash crops allows people to earn an income.

Bad results

- Rivers or other water sources can be polluted. This makes people sick or kills the fish they use for food.
- When soils are damaged, they do not grow healthy crops.

Roads

Here is what happens when a road is built.

- People can get goods to and from markets and have a better life.
- People can get to health services quickly.
- The road environment becomes more dangerous for pedestrians and some wildlife.
- Exotic plants can colonise the edge of the road.
- Water can run off the road and flood gardens if drainage is poor.

For you to try

Discuss your rural environment.

- What are the good things about it?
- What are the problems, or the bad things about it?
- Write a report to show what could be done to improve your local rural environment.

Population density

Population density is the average number of people living in a square kilometre. The population density in much of rural Papua New Guinea is low. This is because it is hard to live in many parts of the country. Some places are too steep. Some are too wet, and some are very isolated. The highest rural population density is in the central Highland valleys.

Cities have the highest population density. Cities continue to grow because people move from rural areas to cities. They want to be close to services that will make living easier.

Papua New Guinea now has over five million people. The population is growing rapidly.

For you to try

- Is the population increasing in your community? Use census figures to find out. What impacts do you think a growing population will have on your environment?
- Choose a feature of your environment and show how people have changed it. You could use a diagram, drawing or write a paragraph. Then make lists of the good and bad results coming from the changes.
- Ask your parents, grandparents and other adults about traditional ways of protecting the environment. Make a list of these traditional ways. Then discuss in class: 'Are the traditional ways of protecting the community environment working?'
- Why do you think it has been made illegal to fish with dynamite or derris root? Why do you think that using rotenone or dieldrin to fish is even worse?
- Find out what laws there are in your community to protect the environment. Make a list of the laws. Then discuss in class: 'Are the laws working?'

The environment provides natural resources. Natural resources are something of value from nature, like trees or oil. It is something that can be taken and sold without many changes. Industries such as mining, forestry and fisheries take natural resources. Water and air are two of the most important natural resources on earth.

What is sustainable use of the environment?

To sustain means to maintain something so it can keep going. If we sustain the environment we use it, but we don't use all of it.

What would happen if we cut all the trees down and there were no more forests? Some of the results would be:

- There would be no more timber to build houses or other buildings, or to make school desks, furniture and many other things.
- There would be frequent flooding and erosion. There would be more muddy water because there would be no forests to help absorb and slow the movement of the water.
- Most butterflies, many types of birds and many types of animals would disappear because their homes had been destroyed.
- All the different forest products that produce medicines and food would disappear.

But what would happen if we did not use the forest or cut any down trees at all?

- We couldn't build traditional houses and there would be no timber for other types of buildings.
- Many places could not practice slash-and-burn agriculture and there would be little land to grow crops.
- People would not be allowed to hunt and eat animals found in the forest.
- Some people would start to illegally use the forest.
- Some people would not have jobs.

Both situations are bad. So, how do we use the forest without using it all up? Or how do we sustain the use of our forests?

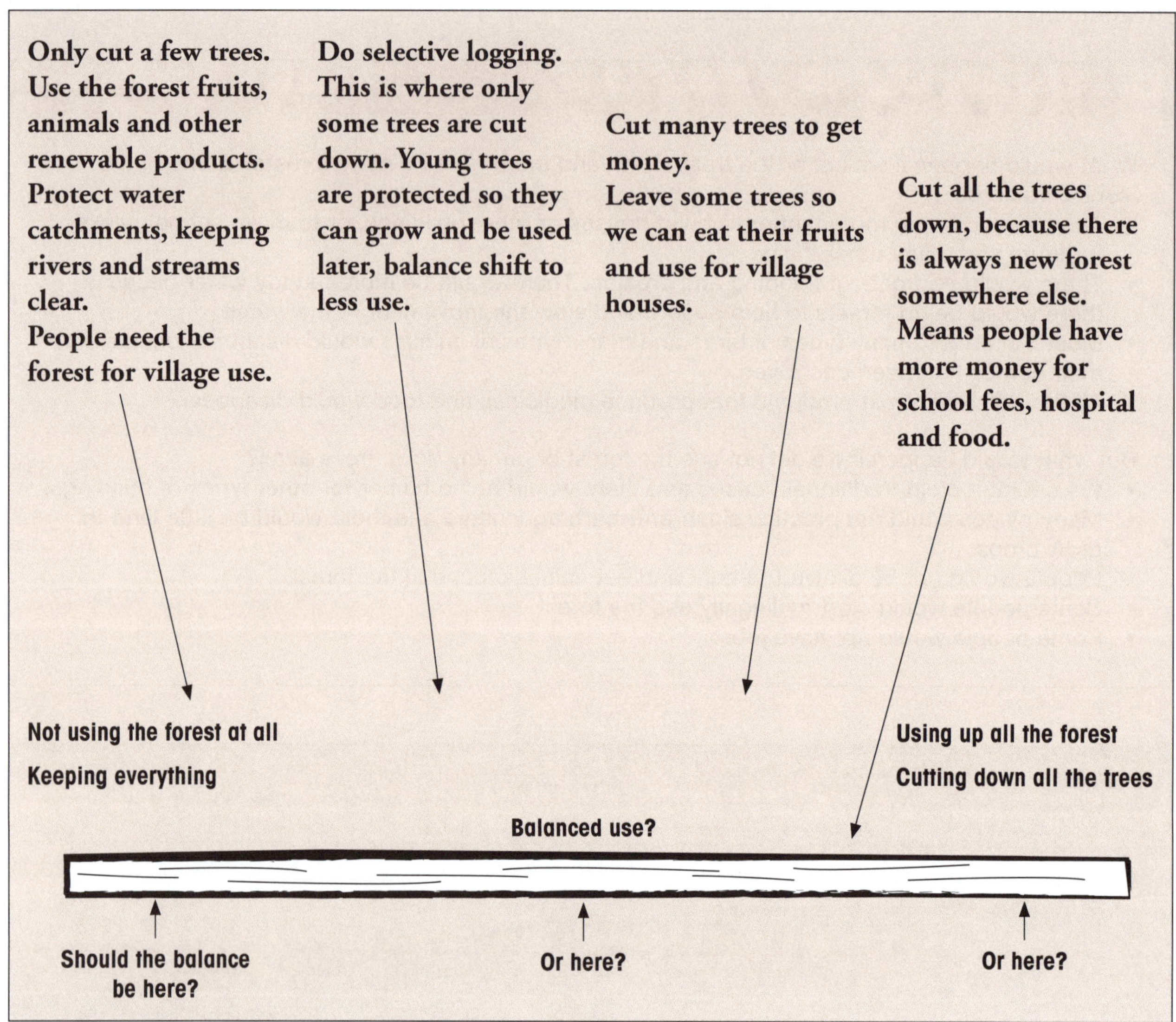

Where should the balance be?

Sustainable use is somewhere between the two extremes. Finding the right balance can be very difficult. People have different ideas about how to do this. Making money quickly and the needs of growing populations often influence how the environment is used or misused.

For you to try

- Look at the diagram on this page. Where do you think the balance should be for using the forests? Explain your reasoning to the class.
- Choose some use of the environment, land, river or sea and make a balance diagram for it. Explain to the class why you have chosen to put the balance point in where you have.

Ramu Sugar set to expand in palm

RAMU Sugar Limited (RSL) will plant 10 000 hectares of oil palm in the Ramu Valley with 2 000 hectares expected by 2006. Their plan moved a step closer to realisation with the approval of the company's environment plan by the Minister for Environment and Conservation.

The company chairman said, "We are looking at planting up to 2 000 hectares of oil palm between 2005 and 2006 … The landowners have approached us showing interest to grow oil palm and we are involving the landowners to plant and this includes the nurseries."

He said Ramu Sugar Limited had its reforestation plan that would see the company planting different varieties of trees where the forest would be cleared.

"Ramu Sugar will be here for a long time and our plan is to plant 10 million trees of different varieties."

Extracted from the *Post-Courier* 9 Feb 2004

For you to try

- Read the newspaper article. How is Ramu Sugar trying to balance its use of land?

Renewable and non-renewable resources

When we look at sustainable development we need to consider renewable and non-renewable resources.

Renewable resources are those resources that will continue to be replaced, if we look after them. Examples include the forest, fisheries, water and agriculture. Sources of power that are renewable include solar power from sunlight, wind, hydropower and tides.

Non-renewable resources are those resources that, once taken out of the land, are not replaced. Once minerals like copper, gold and oil have been removed from the ground, no more can be mined. These are non-renewable

For you to try

- Invite a guest speaker to your class to talk about the wise use of non-renewable resources. How can they help to sustain development?

NATURAL HAZARDS AND THE ENVIRONMENT

Natural means a part of nature. A hazard is something dangerous. Natural hazards are part of the environment. Examples of natural hazards are cyclones, drought, earthquakes, fire, floods, frost, landslides, tsunamis and volcanic eruptions. Different parts of Papua New Guinea face different natural hazards.

People learn to live with natural hazards when they happen often. Parts of Papua New Guinea have droughts every year so people have learned how to live with these. Buildings and houses can be made to survive earthquakes or cyclones. Careful planning or traditions may keep people from settling on floodplains or in places where tsunamis are common.

Natural hazards that do not happen very often can cause problems. People have forgotten they occur or do not know what to do. People can learn to live with natural hazards in some places.

People can create or add to the risk of nature's hazards by poor management. People can cause flooding and landslides by:

- cutting down vegetation
- dumping waste material on slopes
- clearing unstable, steep slopes.

When people change the environment they can increase the risk of natural hazards. Drought and storms may be increasing because of global warming that is caused by human activities.

Mountain dangers

Landslides and flash floods are natural hazards of mountain areas. Landslides are caused by a large amount of soil sliding down steep slopes. They are a danger in mountainous and steep areas. Earthquakes, volcanoes and heavy rainfall can cause soil to slide suddenly.

Very heavy rain can also cause rivers to rise quickly. This can create a wave of water that roars down the river. People in the Highlands and in coastal places near the mountain catchments must be careful of flash flooding.

Coastal dangers

Some natural hazards only occur along parts of the coast. For example, tsunamis are very large waves from the sea. They can wash away entire villages. Earthquakes beneath the sea cause tsunamis.

Another coastal hazard is cyclones. These are very large storms formed at sea.

For you to try

- Draw posters about natural hazards in your community and how your community deals with them.

Living with natural hazards

Look at the list of natural hazards in the table. Then answer the questions that follow the table. Ask elders for added information and collect people's different stories. Share with the class.

Natural Hazard	Types of long-term protection How can we live with this hazard?		What can you do if caught in this hazard?
Cyclones	Strengthen buildings and roofs. Avoid building in low-lying areas that are cyclone-prone. Provide cyclone warning systems so people can leave before the storm.	→	Listen to weather warnings. Leave the area if possible. Leave weak houses and buildings. Lie in open areas or seek shelter in caves or shelter in cyclone-proof buildings. When a cyclone hit Tufi in Oro Province in the 1970s people had no choice but to run and lie on open ground until the storm passed. Houses were blown down and huge trees were flattened in the forest on the nearby volcano.
Drought	Use water conservation programs. Use appropriate crops and mulch. Protect water catchments. Use traditional water sources as in past droughts.	→	Use water carefully. Turn off taps in urban areas and only use water outside for food crops. Apply dry farming methods. For example, the Motu use stone mulching in the dry season for some plants (that is, they put large stones around the plants to help keep moisture in the soil).
Earthquakes	Strengthen buildings. Design buildings to be flexible. Some traditional Papua New Guinea houses are flexible enough to withstand an earthquake. Some concrete and brick buildings have had problems.	→	Stand in a doorway, get under your desk or go outside away from buildings. Do not panic. People were hurt in the 1979 Port Moresby earthquake because they ran and bumped into each other. Panic, not the earthquake, hurt them. Some jumped into lifts (elevators) in buildings. This is not a good idea in any emergency because the power may fail.
Fire	Be very careful when burning off and making fires. Land clearing by burning is a global hazard.	→	Avoid very thick smoke. Do not try to run uphill. Seek a safe place until the fire passes.
Floods	Protect water catchments and riverbanks. Trees and bushes help slow floodwaters. Planning or traditions that prohibit building on flood plains help stop some flood problems. Another solution is houses built on stilts. Floods are part of the natural cycle of rivers. It is a way of feeding the soil in flood areas. Many types of wildlife and plants depend on flooding.	→	Do not try to cross rivers or streams when they are flooded. Stay away from rivers, streams and flood areas during times of heavy rains or when you can see heavy rain in the mountains. Parts of Papua New Guinea flood every year and people have learned to live with this hazard (but it is harder with modern vehicles and some modern buildings).

Hazard	Prevention		Response
Frost	Choose frost-resistant crops. Small gardens can be covered for protection. Listen to weather forecasts.	→	Wear warm clothes.
Landslips	Carefully choose locations for settlements. Protect the trees and bushes on unstable steep slopes. Remember that tectonic forces created steep mountains. It is natural for them to come down. Often they erode slowly but they can change quickly too. So don't settle where the mountain might fall down.	→	Sometimes you can hear roots snapping just before a landslip starts. Leave the area immediately. Be careful when it rains for a long time. Stay away from problem areas in times of heavy rains.
Lightning	Use lightning rods or other devices to earth electricity in case lightning strikes a house or building.	→	Do not shelter under a big tree if caught outside. Keep body low to ground. Do not hold metal umbrellas, steel spears or iron bars. If hair starts to attract electricity, run away quickly.
Tsunamis	Early warning systems can monitor earthquake activity at sea. Traditional elders and planning authorities can warn people of dangerous areas to settle.	→	Move to high ground as quickly as you can if the sea suddenly goes out. Sometimes you will see fish flapping on the sand.
Volcanic Eruptions	Early warning systems like the one in Rabaul monitor volcanic activity. But think a little more about Rabaul. Was it a good idea to build a city inside a volcano? It is a very beautiful place with rich volcanic soils but the location carries a price. Another solution is not to settle in the area. But, like floods, volcanoes can feed the soil with ash. This makes it very good for gardens.	→	Evacuate the area before it is too late. Some volcanoes can be natural hazards even when they are not erupting if you go inside the crater. Several tourists have died climbing into Matapit volcano near Rabaul when poison gas leaked out.

For you to try

- What advice do older people have for surviving a natural hazard?
- How did people deal with this hazard traditionally?
- What has changed in how your community might deal with the hazard today?
- How many of these hazards have been experienced by at least one person in your community?
- Challenge: Can the class find someone with a story for each of the hazards listed?

Maps

A map is a representation of all or part of Earth's surface. Maps help us explore parts of our environment.

1. Maps can display features of the physical environment.

2. Maps can show features of the human environment.

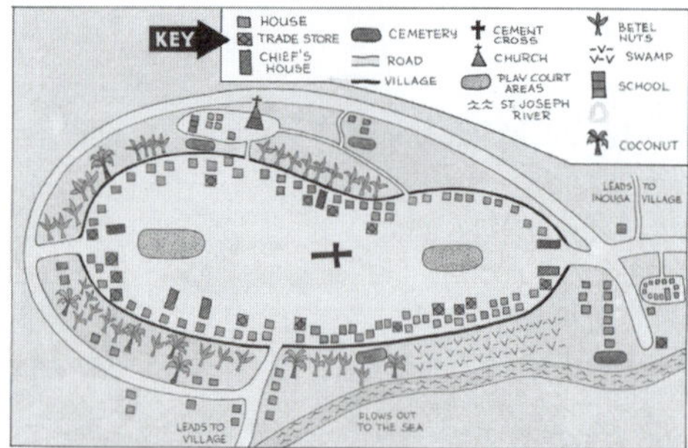

3. Maps can also show features of both the human and natural environment. These are called topographic maps. Topographic maps are common in Papua New Guinea. They use contour lines to show the elevation and shape of the land.

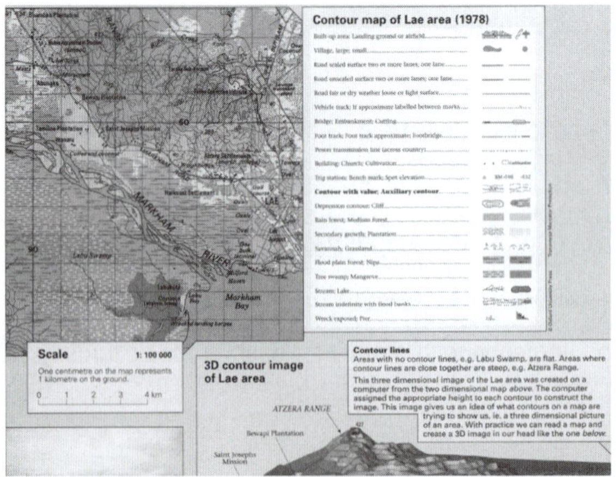

How to use and read maps

There are three important things to consider when you look at a map. They are:

- orientation
- scale
- key.

Orientation

The orientation is the direction of the map. The orientation of standard maps is NORTH.

When you are using a map it is best to orient the map and your body with what is on the ground. This means holding the map with its features in the same way that you are looking at the features on the ground.

This girl has oriented her map to the same way she is looking at the ground. This makes the map easier to read.

Scale

Some maps cover little distances. Other maps cover large distances. The scale of a map lets you measure distances on the map. The scale is a line or rule with measurements. A measurement on the line matches a certain distance on the ground.

Scales are also given as ratios. Usually the ratio is one unit on the map matches a certain number of units on the ground.

Scale: 1:100 000

This means that one unit on the map is 100 000 units on the ground. In this scale one centimetre (cm) on the map equals 100 000 centimetres on the ground. 100 000 centimetres is the same as one kilometre (km). So 5cm on the map is 5km on the ground.

For you to try

- If you travel 12cm on the map, how far will you travel on the ground?
- If you travel a quarter of a metre on the map, how far will you travel on the ground?

Key

The key to a map tells you what features are on it. Here is a key to a topographical map. Look at the different features. Some are human and others are part of the natural environment.

The map also shows contour lines. These help you understand the landforms. The contour lines are showing you the elevation or height of the landforms. Where the lines are close together it means that it is very steep. Lines that are further apart show a gentler slope that will be easier to walk or drive up.

For you to try

- Draw a map of your school. Include all buildings and major features in the school grounds. Design specific symbols to represent these features on your map.
- List these symbols in a key below your map.

Organisation

Chapter summary

In this chapter you will have an opportunity to:

- ✓ look at the organisation of society and of the economy
- ✓ learn what a local community is and the types of groups that might be in it
- ✓ gain information about roles, rights and responsibilities
- ✓ determine what attitudes and values are
- ✓ distinguish between attitudes and values
- ✓ realise that roles, attitudes and values can change.

Syllabus references

Strand: Organisation

Substrand: Social and Economic Organisation

Outcomes

Students are able to:

6.2.1 identify the main features of local groups and the contributions they make to the local society and economy

6.2.2: appraise the relationship between groups and the contributions they make to the local society and economy

6.2.3 participate in local social and economic activities that contribute to the development of the local community.

SOCIAL ORGANISATION

We can study social organisation by looking at different groups that make up our society. People are all around us in groups.

Today, for example, have you seen groups of people at play or groups of people doing work? Consider the group you are in right now, studying and learning.

Think of how many groups there are around the world doing different things. People form groups because human beings are social beings. To be social is to be part of a group. In a group, we depend on each other. These groups can include families, communities or societies.

There are many different types of groups. Here are a few examples.

Sports team

Teacher and children in schools

Families

Most people like to communicate and network. To communicate is to talk and listen, write and discuss. People, newspapers and movies communicate. To network is to meet more people. Networking is meeting the friends of your friends or finding out about your cousin's friends.

Hermits live alone with little communication and no networking.

For you to try

- How many different groups can you find in your local community?
- Write the name of each group and its purpose.
- Discuss the ways these groups communicate and network.
- Below are examples of groups. Remember that your groups and purposes may be very different.

Group name	Purposes
Lik lik stoa	Sell goods, make money, be in business, keep busy
Volleyball teams	Play a sport, exercise, make friends, have fun
Evening prayer group	Worship, get together, fellowship, share food
Families	Raise children, support the community and…?

What is a group?

A group is a number of people who have something in common. For example, a group may be people from the same place, or people who share the same values.

Primary groups are small and people in these groups stick together. Families, clans and some villages in Papua New Guinea are primary groups. Generally they last for years, or even lifetimes.

Secondary groups can be much larger. Some secondary groups may also last for a long time. They are a more recent idea in Papua New Guinea. Secondary groups can be institutions or associations.

An institution consists of many different groups of people all doing a particular job so that the institution can work. The Department of Health is an institution. It consists of groups such as doctors, nurses, administrators, field officers and maintenance people.

An association can be less formal. A sporting group or a political support group are examples of associations.

What is the local community?

The local community is your local place and the people who live there. There are two main locations for communities in Papua New Guinea — rural and urban. Most communities are rural. Villages and stations are rural. Cities and large towns are urban locations.

GROUPS IN LOCAL COMMUNITIES

Local communities are made up of many different groups. These groups may work together in different ways. Sometimes they cooperate and other times they may compete. Let's start to look at the way people group themselves. Here are some of the groups you may find in a local community:

- Family
- Clan
- All male or all female groups
- Age groups — where groups are limited to certain ages
- Ethnic groups — often called wantoks in Papua New Guinea
- Social services — institutions like health and education
- Social and recreational activities — often associations
- Religion
- Economic activity
- Local government
- And remember, your local society is a group too.

For you to try

Answer the following questions and write answers on the blackboard.

- Which gender group are you in? Do you act differently if you are one or the other? Do you like doing different things?
- What about your age? What age group are you in? Do you think you will be thinking the same when you are older? Or will your ideas change? In what age group are your parents?
- What about important ideas? How do you know if something is good or bad? And why do you like some things and not others?
- How many definitions of community can you find? Collect them and compare them in class. Then ask yourself, 'Am I a member in all the different definitions of communities?'

Family

Family is the basic group in a local community. Families start with marriage. It gives social or group recognition to the couple. The wedding ceremony shows the community that the couple is serious. Ceremonies show the roles and values in a culture.

Different types of wedding ceremonies occur in Papua New Guinea today. Some couples are married in churches while others are married in traditional ceremonies. Some couples are married by government officers in civil weddings. Other wedding ceremonies may have a mix of traditional and introduced parts. For example, traditional feasts often follow church weddings.

A major role for families is to have children. This is so important in Papua New Guinea that some societies will give children to a couple when they are just starting out. In other cases, a couple will be given children if they cannot produce their own.

For you to try

- Collect pictures or make drawings of wedding ceremonies in your community. Label them to show what parts are still traditional and what parts have been introduced.

Nuclear and extended families

Social scientists often identify two types of family.

- One is the nuclear family. It is made up of parents and children only. Nuclear families tend to be more common in urban environments.
- The other type of family is called the extended family. Besides parents and children, it includes others such as grandparents, aunties, uncles and cousins. The extended family may all live together.

The different cultures and environments in Papua New Guinea lead to different types of families. All of them produce valuable members of society. Everyone in a family has certain roles, rights and responsibilities. You must be careful when you study families to avoid bias and prejudice.

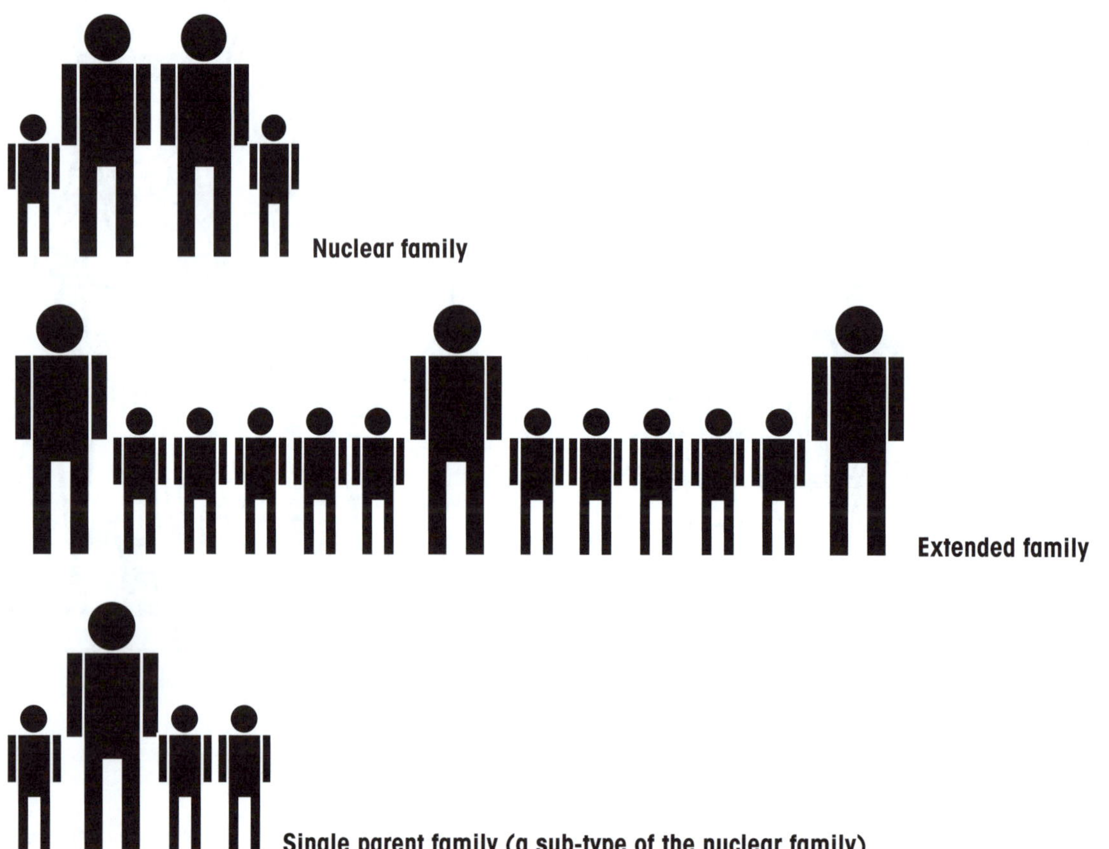

For you to try

- As a class, discuss the types of families that you can find in your community.
- At home, ask your parents what the most important family values are. Write them down and bring your work to school. Compare these family values with your classmates. Are the values similar or are there differences?

  How do you think these family values assist the community?

Kinship

Kinship means people who are related to each other by marriage or descent. English uses terms like brother, sister, mother, father, uncle and aunt. In Papua New Guinea, different communities have different ways of looking at kin.

Clan

One large grouping of kin is the clan. There are clans found in many parts of rural Papua New Guinea. Clan membership is important to land rights for that group. There can be disputes between clans and disputes within clans over land.

People can be taken into clans. Their families may have worked for generations of the clan. The clan value was to add good people to the clan, even if they were not born into it. Today, some people try to change this value. They don't want to share the land or royalties. This causes problems in the clan.

Land rights and other rights in a family or clan may be organised as matrilineal or patrilineal. Examples of both systems can be found in Papua New Guinea.

- Matrilineal means that the land rights come through the mother. There are matrilineal systems on Trobriand and Misima islands.
- In patrilineal systems the rights come through the father. There are many different patrilineal systems in the Highlands.

For you to try

- See how many clans you can locate in your community. Hold a class discussion on the role of clans in your community. Then see how many clan values you can list.
- Discuss the land right systems found in your rural community. If you are in an urban community, discuss how land rights have changed. Discuss what land rights people still have and how values about land rights are changing.

Gender specific and age groups

There are groups that are based on the sex of the person. They are only for males or only for females. They can also be called gender specific groups. There are also groups based on age. There can be groups based on both the sex of the person and their age.

Traditionally men and women had many separate groups based on the sex of the person (gender) and age. The men's house, the haus tamboran, initiation ceremonies and certain types of singsings have traditionally been separated by gender and/or age. Newer divisions based on gender and age include some sporting groups, and parts of the police and military. Your school class is an age group.

For you to try

- Look at the following pictures and discuss the role of gender and age in each. How important are gender and age in your local community?

Roles

A role is what a person is expected to do in different social positions. A role may be teaching, learning, setting an example, sharing, providing food for a family or healing sick people.

At school, your role is that of student. Your role is to learn. Your teacher has a role too. The teacher's role is to teach.

When you are in the market buying something, you are acting in a role. The role of a buyer in many Papua New Guinea markets is to compare the same product and find the best one. Setting the price is not part of the buyer's role. Being a seller is another role. The seller's role is to set the price and sell the product.

The roles of buyer and seller can change in different communities.

For you to try

- What is the role of a big man in Papua New Guinea? Is it helping people? Is it representing a group or groups in community meetings? What different things do you think it includes? Discuss your answers with the class.

Rights and responsibilities

Every role has rights and responsibilities. For example, a teacher in a government school is responsible for teaching you. A teacher's role has many other responsibilities. The teacher is also responsible to see that you are not harmed. The teacher should also keep order in the classroom.

The role also carries rights. Being paid is a teacher's right. Respect from students and parents is another teacher's right.

Rights are what you get as part of a role. A student has the right to go to school. Your community or group accepts these rights. Responsibilities are the other part of the role. These are the actions your community or group expects from you. A student's responsibility is to study.

Sometimes a role is taken away if people do not perform their responsibilities. At other times, a group or community may criticise how a person acts in a role. This is called social pressure.

Being a citizen of Papua New Guinea is a role.

Multiple roles

The same person may have several roles. A person may have the role of mother, businesswoman, Sunday school teacher, daughter and wife all at the same time. What if this person then became a widow instead of a wife? Can you see how the role changes?

In Papua New Guinea, kinship roles are still very important in many places. Consider the role of uncle, aunt, cousin, father, mother, father-in-law and mother-in-law. These roles are still very important because family and clan groups provide so much support and help each other. There are many more tok ples terms for kin than in English.

Here is an example of one person with three roles.

Mother
Rights: respect from children, support from husband
Responsibilities: caring for young children, preparing food for family

Businesswoman
Rights: Share in tradestore profit, respect from customers
Responsibilities: running tradestore, paying charges and taxes

Sunday school teacher:
Rights: respect in the Church, place to sit for teaching
Responsibilities: protection of the children in her care, teaching religion

For you to try

- Role play: people often do role play to learn about problems and issues. They will pretend they are in some one else's role and act out a situation. Their rights and responsibilities determine how they act.
- In class make a list of the different roles you can identify in your community. For example you might find tradestore owner, doctor, businessman, widow, mother, farmer, PMV driver and more.
- Complete your list. Cut the paper up so that each role is on a separate piece of paper. Place them in a box, bag or hat. Divide the class into two teams. A team member doing the role play draws out a piece of paper (only that person sees the role). The other team asks, 'Tell us one of your rights and one of your responsibilities'. The role player does this and the other team guesses the role. If they are wrong they can continue to ask for more rights and responsibilities. The game progresses with a person on the other team drawing out a role. The game finishes when all the roles in your community have been acted out.

Attitudes and values

The attitudes and values of a group of people should tell us how they might behave in different situations.

Attitudes

Attitudes are the way you feel about things. Attitudes can be liking or not liking something. Maybe you like studying English but you don't like making fires. Maybe you like living in the village but don't think you would like to live in the city.

People may have attitudes about work and play. Some people love to work. Other people have a different attitude and don't like work. They might prefer to play.

People's attitudes can change quickly. This can happen in things like politics. People may like a political party very much on Wednesday. If bad news comes, their attitude changes. They do not like that same political party on Saturday.

For you to try

Divide the class into two groups. Make one group all boys and the other all girls. The groups are to discuss their attitudes about boys and girls.

There are four questions for each group:

- What do you like about girls? (List the five most important.)
- What do you like about boys? (List five.)
- What don't you like about boys? (List five.)
- What don't you like about girls? (List five.)

The groups give the teacher the lists. The teacher summarises the answers on the board and the class discusses the answers.

- Are boys and girls' attitudes different?
- What might make some of these attitudes change?
- Are values included in the answers? Are values changing?

Please keep the answers from this exercise as we shall use it again soon. (See page 57.)

Values

Values are stronger than attitudes. They are beliefs that do not change quickly. (But they can change and often do change over time.) Honesty and telling the truth about important things are values. Helping a wantok is another value. Making sacrifices so your children can have an education represents another value.

People in the same group often share the same values. For example, teachers in a school may all value education. They may value study and books. They may, however, have different attitudes about some students. Or they may value books, but have different attitudes about particular books.

For you to try

- How many roles do you have? Make a list of all your roles and the rights and responsibilities that go with them. Be sure to think about all the roles you have in your community.
- Then divide a page into four parts and in each part draw a picture of yourself in a role. Write beneath each picture what you think an important value in this role might be.

You could do this on one piece of paper like this:

Role: Sporting hero, soccer
Value: Winning at any cost
(Is this really your value?)

Role: Big sister
Value: Protecting little brother and sister from harm

Use both sides of the paper and you can draw up to eight roles. Maybe you have even more?

Changing roles, attitudes and values

Roles, attitudes and values are changing in our communities.

Young people used to value old people in their community. The old people had wisdom and understood the environment.

Now the old people's role is changing in many communities. Some young people don't listen or learn from old people now. They think that the old people have nothing to teach them. They don't value the traditional knowledge.

Another change in roles, attitudes and values is in taking care of old people. In Australia and other Western countries many old people go to old people's homes. Their family no longer takes care of them. In Papua New Guinea the family role still includes taking care of the old. This can change, however, if young people move away to work in the city. In some cases they stop sending money to help the old people at home.

For you to try

- Discuss this example in class. A woman married a man who was a coffee grower. He sent her to study business and accounts. He paid for her studies. When she returned she could help him make his coffee business bigger. And she now does all the banking. What new roles does she have? Do you think some of her attitudes changed while she did her studies?

Melanesian values

Some of the most important values for Melanesians are about land and land ownership. Melanesian landownership is group ownership.

Melanesian attitudes and values are very different from Western values about land. This has led to conflict and misunderstanding in the past. We can still find many examples of conflicting values about land today in Papua New Guinea.

Giving generously is a Melanesian value. In Melanesian values the big man or the rich man gives much more than an ordinary person. This shows that he is a big man. But all people who receive gifts should pay back with their own gifts or services later. Receiving gifts and giving gifts back is called gift exchange. You should have many examples to share with the class.

Payback for injury, loss or death is another Melanesian value. This leads to cycles of violence that can be broken by compensation. With compensation we see values changing. Money has now become the most important means of compensation.

Cycle of violence

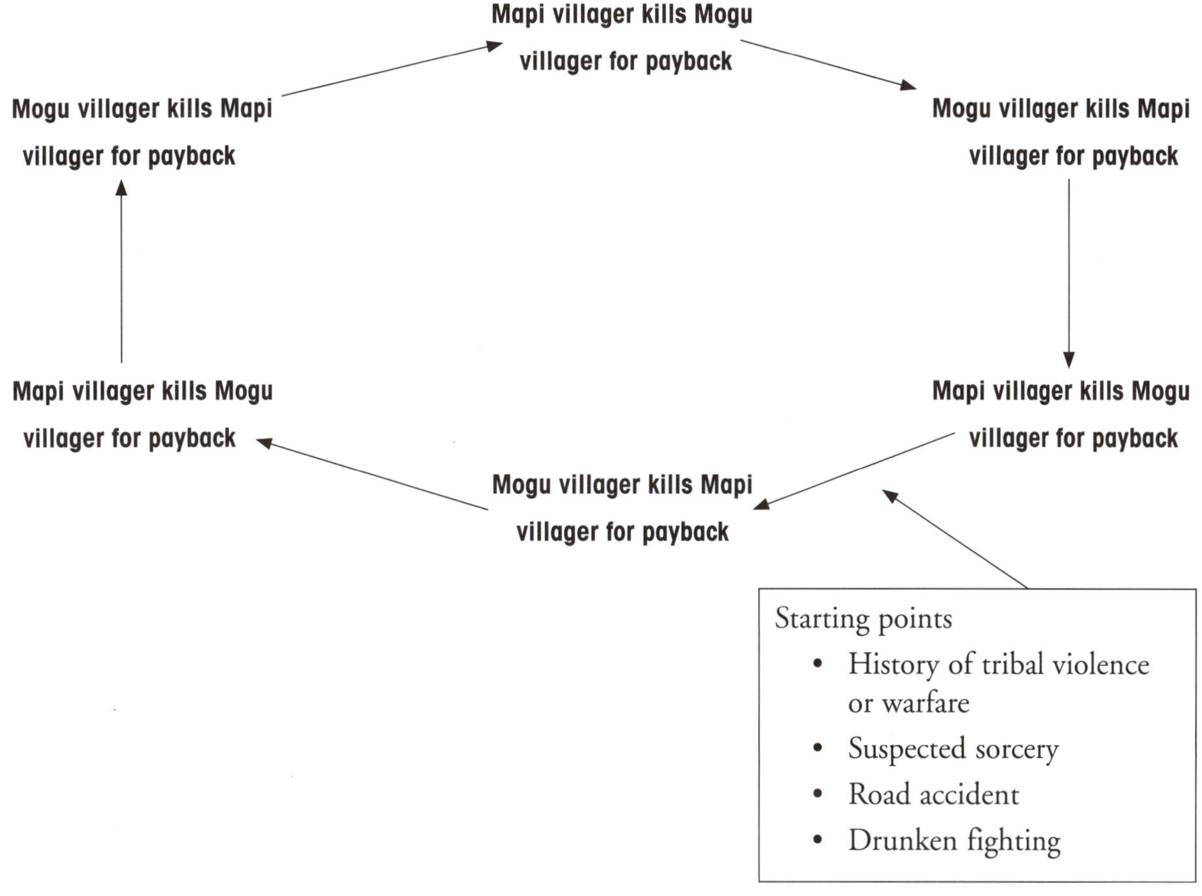

Starting points

- History of tribal violence or warfare
- Suspected sorcery
- Road accident
- Drunken fighting

A cycle is a circle. You can see how the cycle of violence will continue like a circle unless it is broken. Prejudice, bias and some values can make it very hard to break. Compensation is one way to break the cycle.

Payback and the problems of violence lead to another Melanesian value. This is to avoid argument. If you do not argue you will not fight. If you do not fight there can be no cycle of violence. People will often agree or say yes even when they mean no. This avoids a fight.

It can cause communication problems if people do not understand that people are agreeing so they can avoid an argument. This value often does not work when people drink alcohol.

For you to try

- What Melanesian values can you find in your community? Write them on a list.
- How do these values affect the roles that people have in the community?
- How do these values affect different groups in the community?

Villagers threaten to close airport

Villagers in a province are threatening to shut down the airport and a portion of the main highway.

The threat was made by disgruntled villagers after a reserve policeman attached to the police station allegedly mobilised some men and bashed youths from the village in retaliation following the death of a man who was killed in a road accident.

The man was allegedly under the influence and died after falling off a truck belonging to a man from the village Village community leaders allege that the police reservist, who is also a relative of the deceased, has been threatening their villagers and led a group of men to the Police Station where they assaulted nine youths from the village who were taken to the station for questioning after the accident.

A villager said the youths were severely beaten and taken to the General Hospital for treatment before being locked up for seven days without being charged.

He described the detention as illegal and a violation of their human rights.

He called for an investigation to be carried out into the actions of the reserve policeman.

He said the driver of the truck was charged for driving an unregistered and uninsured motor vehicle. He said the villagers were also forced to pay K5,000 in cash and kind to the deceased's relatives although they were not responsible for his death. He said the policeman and his gang are also demanding K45,000 as well as the truck and a PMV bus from the villagers.

The villagers own the land which the airport is on.

Abridged and extracted from *The National* 5 Jan 2004

For you to try

1. Read this extract from the newspaper. Answer these questions:

- List the Melanesian values that you can find in this article.
- List any introduced values that you can find.
- How many different roles can you find in the article? Make a list.
- What rights and responsibilities do these roles have?
- What multiple roles can you find? Can you find any conflicts in the rights and responsibilities of a person who has a multiple role?

2. Draw a diagram of the situation using the above information. Show the cycle of conflict and the different ways it might be broken. Label the parts as:

- Traditional
- Not traditional (or introduced)
- Partly traditional

For example, traditional compensation uses special gifts. Compensation in cash is partly traditional. An investigation and violation of human rights is not traditional. It is introduced.

3. Investigate a case of conflict in your community and explore ways to break the cycle of violence. You can draw a diagram using the previous diagram as a model, or the class can try to solve it through role play.

Being careful about attitudes

We need to be careful with attitudes and values. Wrong attitudes can cause problems when you are studying the community. Two big problems are:

- **bias**
- **prejudice.**

Let's look at these problems and what we can do about them.

Prejudice

Prejudice means to judge before you know any of the facts. For example, you decide you do not like something before you can really know the truth. A child will look at a plate of food and say 'yuck' without even trying it. That is prejudice.

More seriously, people may be prejudiced against certain groups or types of other people without even knowing them. Maybe their skin is a different colour, or they come from a different place.

PREJUDICE

I don't like those people from Fish Village.

They are no good. They don't wash.

They're lazy!

PREJUDICE

I don't like those people from Crab Village

They are no good. They don't wash.

They're lazy!

You can find many examples of prejudice. Everyone has some prejudices. Often this is because you have not thought about an attitude. You learned it from someone else and just accepted it.

This can happen in groups. People accept the group's prejudice without thinking. Maybe the two villages on page 54 were enemies many years ago. Now that has changed, but the attitude has not. It is a prejudiced attitude.

A prejudiced value is very serious and hurts people. Here is an example. Someone says (or thinks) I am not giving that person a job because:

- she is a woman and women are not as good as men
- he is from Enga and they are no good
- she is from Daru and they are no good
- he is from Central and they are no good
- she is from Buka and they are no good
- he is too old and old people are not as good as young people.

All such statements are seriously prejudiced. When gathering information about an idea (or question) you must be careful of prejudice. First check yourself. Are you open minded? Can you accept that your idea may be right or wrong? Then listen carefully to all the people you speak to. There will always be at least two sides to any story.

For you to try

- Discuss in class the common prejudices found in your community. You can start with the school. Are there any prejudices? Discuss the problems that prejudice causes. How can you make things better? Try an example through role play.

Bias

Bias means liking or favouring something unfairly. If a company making bread employs ten men and just one woman, you could say it is biased towards hiring men. The women could do the work. (They are probably also prejudiced against women.)

Sometimes bias can be mild. You might say, I am biased towards wearing blue clothes. That is not a big problem. It becomes a big problem if you make everyone else wear blue clothes.

Have you seen people arguing over how to do things? Each person will want to do it their own way. Often this is bias. When you look closely, there are many ways a person can do things. Generally you may think that your way is better. Groups are very strong in this type of biased thinking. Groups often think they are the best. This can show both bias and prejudice.

Here is how an example of how bias works in groups.

- For a while, a young teacher left Papua New Guinea and went to Indonesia.
- Papua New Guineans have their own way to fasten a lap lap.
- People in Indonesia laughed at the teacher's Papua New Guinea way of fastening a lap lap. Men in Indonesia tie their lap laps differently to Papua New Guinea.
- Some people insisted on tying it again for him in the Indonesian way. They have a bias for the Indonesian way and a bias against the Papua New Guinea way.
- Really, both ways are just as good but groups often think that only their way is best.

Here are two ways to tie a lap lap. Both work just as well but people are biased towards doing it their way.

It is very important to collect all the facts. That means listening to everyone's ideas and being fair. Everyone in the community is important. Sometimes we forget that and are biased. It is important to listen to the elders, to community leaders and other important people. But we also need to hear from those who are not important, the ordinary people and those who can be hidden. Only this way will we better understand our community.

For you to try

- Discuss in class the exercise you did on page 48 where you explored attitudes between boys and girls. Can you find any examples of bias? Can you find any examples of prejudice?
- Papua New Guinea has many different cultures, religions and peoples. They all live together in one nation. Can you identify biases and prejudices between the different groups? Why is it important for the nation to guard against bias and prejudice?
- Investigate bias and prejudice with your own family. Ask family members if they have experienced bias or prejudice. Collect their stories.
- If you have time, search more widely in your own community for other examples of bias or prejudice. Illustrate and write down the best stories. Make a large poster to display at your school. Be sure to include on the poster the ways that you can avoid being biased or prejudiced when studying the community.

GOVERNMENT

Papua New Guinea has a democratic type of government. That means that Papua New Guinea is a democracy. The citizens of a democracy have rights and responsibilities. Voting is both a right and a responsibility. All adults in Papua New Guinea have the right to vote.

Papua New Guinea has different levels of government. The New Organic Law of 1995 gives people representation at:

- local government level
- district government level
- provincial government level
- national government level.

There are some differences for Bougainville and the National Capital District.

Local government in rural and urban communities

Your local community will have a local government. Councillors are elected in a ward and they elect a chairman and treasurer. The purpose of local government is to assist local development. Different local government councils have very different plans for their communities.

For you to try

- Have the class or groups of students interview different councillors.
- Ask about local government plans and activities for your communities.
- Ask them about the problems of local government.
- Ask what has been the best achievement of the local government.
- Write a report on your findings.
- At age 18 you can vote as a citizen of Papua New Guinea. A wise voter knows about government. Will you know about your government?

Government laws and rules

All societies have laws and rules. Your community will have laws and rules. Some are more important than others. You can often tell how important a law or rule is by the punishment that is given for breaking it. Sometimes, different parts of the community will have different laws and rules. Different groups might consider a law or rule less or more important than other groups in the community. This can lead to conflict.

For you to try

- Who are the most important people in your community for keeping the laws and rules? Are there different groups with different laws and rules?
- How do attitudes and values help people to obey laws and rules?
- What does it mean when people do not obey laws and rules? Are the laws wrong? Are the values wrong? Is something else wrong?

Community services and activities

All local communities provide some types of help for members of the community. This includes health, education, security, welfare, law and order, religious or spiritual needs, leisure, economic activities and some infrastructure. We see differences in the level of these services. We often see this difference between rural and urban communities. Urban communities often have more services.

In the past, families and clans provided many of the basic needs and services. There were many different rules for sharing in different parts of Papua New Guinea, but here is one example:

- A grandmother or uncle may have known healing remedies and special plants for different cures.
- The mother and groups of female kin often educated girls.
- The boys often left home at age seven or eight to live and learn in a men's house.
- Welfare depended on the family and clan.

Parts of this are now changing. There are new services for health and education. Sometimes these come directly from government, or from new religious groups.

1. Primary group

Traditional responsibility

Grandmother made medicines to cure her grandchildren

2. Secondary group

Health institution

Aid post or hospital provides medicine and staff to cure children

In the past, people within communities also depended on each other for security. People took on the role of warrior when fighting other communities. That role still exists. New roles of police and army personnel are working to take over security.

For you to try

- Draw your own examples of changes to community services that compare the past to the present.
- Discuss how the changes to services change values, attitudes and roles.

ECONOMIC ORGANISATION

Economics is the study of wealth and how people make a living. Economists study how wealth is produced and distributed. They ask the question, 'What resources do people have?'

Papua New Guinea has many types of economic systems. We are going to look at the economy of local communities. An economy is based on the resources of a community. In the past people used seashells, salt and pigs for money. Cash, a type of money that uses paper bills and coins, is becoming more important.

Different natural environments affect the economies of local communities. Some communities were located in very difficult environments. Poor soils, too much rain, and malaria made survival difficult. In other environments people found more opportunities to use the resources. People have developed different technologies to survive in all of Papua New Guinea's environments except for the very highest mountain areas.

Today, the newest environment is the urban or city environment.

A village economy in the past

Let's start with an example of a local community. Imagine a village 200 years ago on the coast of Papua New Guinea. Let's call this village Manumanu. Now think, what resources did the people of Manumanu have and how did they make a living?

Labour

The first resource was the people themselves. This resource is called labour or the labour force. People have different skills. In Manumanu the men and women would have had different economic roles. Perhaps the women gardened, collected food and cooked while the men fished and hunted.

Land

To garden or fish, the people needed land. This is another important resource. We count the sea as part of the land. The people of Manumanu would have collected foods and medicines from the forest, hunted animals, taken water from the streams, and made canoes from the trees. The land provided the basis for planting crops. Their clothing and houses came from plants, particularly the pandanus.

- Who do you think made the houses and the clothing?
- Do you think men and women had different economic roles for creating these items?

Technology and capital

Building a house or making a garden requires skills. The people of Manumanu had many different skills. This allowed them to have a good economy that provided food, shelter, protection from their enemies, the means to raise children, and time for other activities. The skills that people have form part of their technology. Different local economies have different technologies.

A good example of a Papua New Guinea technology is the making of bilums. People in different places use different materials to make bilums but the basic technology is the same. Even today there is no machine that can weave a traditional bilum. The bilum weave pulls in two directions to allow a maximum load to be placed in the bilum.

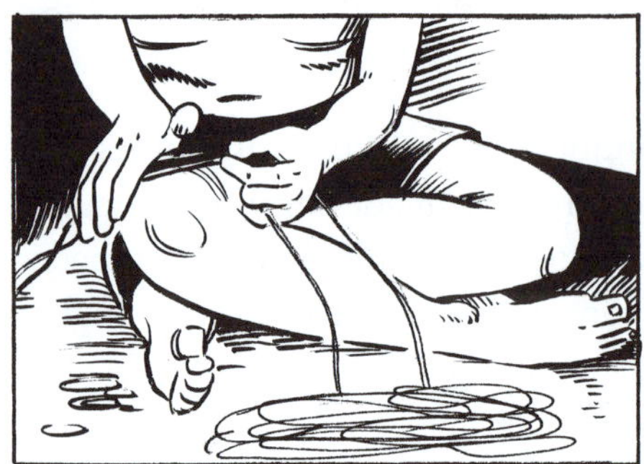

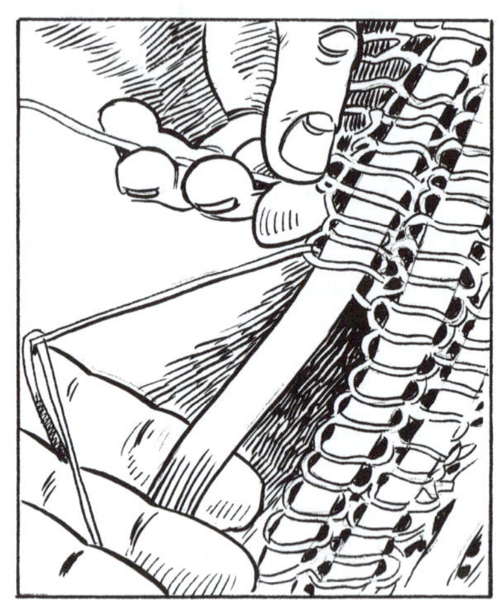

For you to try

- Can you think of other technologies that would be found in Papua New Guinea 200 years ago? Many are so effective they continue to be used today.
- Ask your parents, grandparents and other elders about the technologies of the past. See if you can practise any of them and bring your work to show the class.

How was the local economy in Manumanu organised?

Here is an example from 200 years ago. One night a storm hit the coast and battered Manumanu. Next morning a woman named Kila got up and saw that the family canoe was badly damaged. A big tree had fallen on the canoe. She called to her husband and told him a new canoe would have to be made.

1. First the husband and wife discussed a plan. He knew a good canoe tree on clan land that he could use, but he needed permission from the clan leader. About a year ago he had helped the clan leader make a new house, so the leader owed him and should be glad to say yes.
2. Then the husband needed help to cut the tree down. After it had dried, he would need help to hollow it out and carry it from the forest to the sea.
3. His clan would help him, because he had always helped them before, but Kila would have to prepare food. She would have to make plenty of food so that the helpers could take some home, and some for the clan leader too.
4. There was some surplus in the garden that would be ready, but not enough. Kila would ask a friend for food from her garden. This woman was a cousin and Kila had helped her many times before.

This type of economic organisation relied on family and kin working together. It did not rely on cash (money). It was organised on people trading different resources, including their labour, over time. Much of the traditional economy of Papua New Guinea was based on this economic organisation. It worked for thousands of years and produced large surpluses.

For you to try

- See if you can find examples of economic organisation in Papua New Guinea that do not use cash. Can you still find such examples in your community? Write them up and illustrate your work.

Trade, bartering and scarcity

To make the new canoe, Kila's husband and helpers needed adzes. An adze is similar to a stone axe. Stones to make adzes were scarce in Kila's village. When we say something is scarce, that means there is very little of it. Scarcity is the basis for trade.

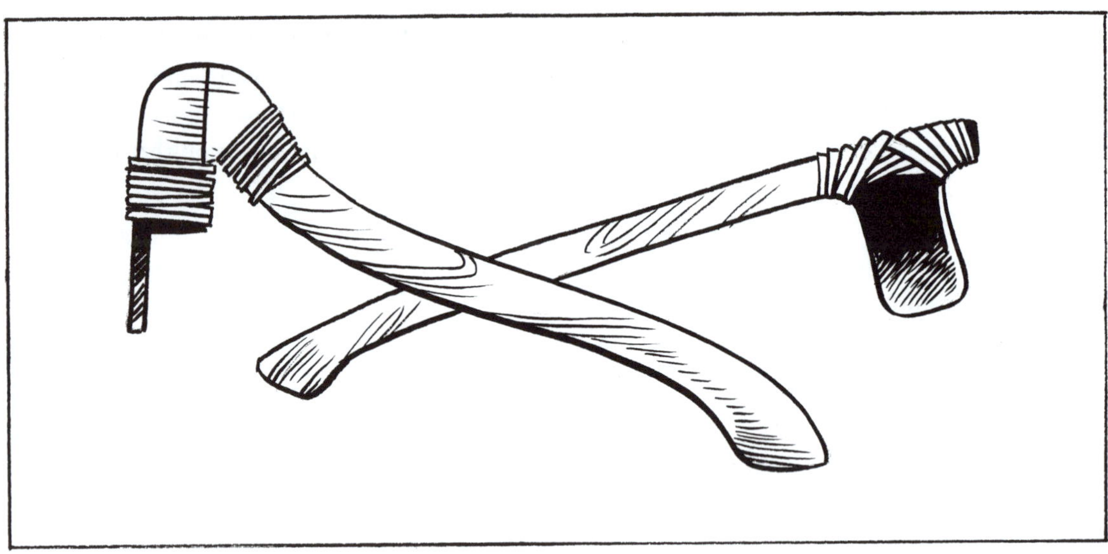

Adzes are similar to stone axes. The best adzes were made from very hard stone. They worked very well and were an important trade item in the traditional economy. Steel axes and chisels have replaced them. The adze technology took three times longer to finish a job than using steel tools. They were very effective in skilled hands; they just took longer to complete a job.

Another village had many good stones for adzes, but didn't have much smoked fish or kina shells. Kila's village had lots of smoked fish and kina shells. So the villages could trade stones for smoked fish and kina shells.

The Manumanu economy was close to self-sufficient. The local community produced most of the items that they needed to survive and live well. The things that the community didn't have could be gained through trade. Trade is another important part of an economy. The trade done by Kila's husband is called barter. A barter economy does not need money.

For you to try

- Students sometimes barter between each other. Have you ever bartered for something?

What was used for money?

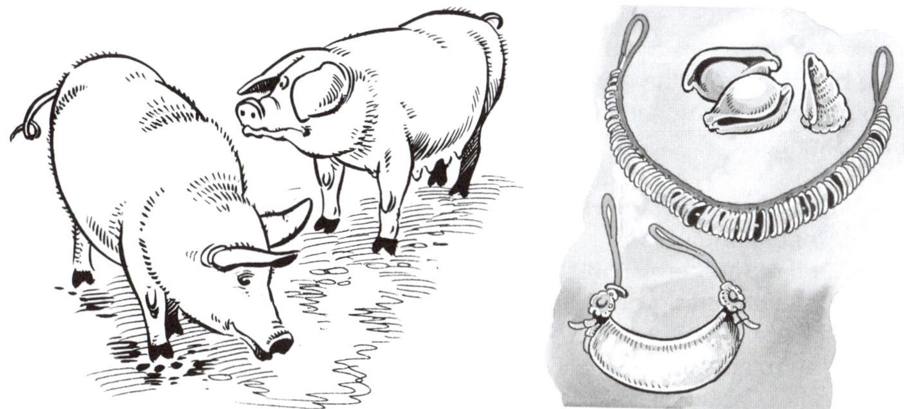

People had no banks. They needed to keep their wealth in other ways. In the Highlands, pigs served as a type of bank. Excess food could go into the pigs, just like putting money into a bank.

Traditional money included items like:

- yams
- kina shells
- shell money.

In the past, salt also served as money.

The Dani people in Indonesian Papua still extract salt in a traditional way high in the mountains.

For you to try

- Look at the examples of traditional money. What was used for traditional money in your community? Ask the older people and see what examples you can find.
- Make pictures or drawings of what used to be traditional money and what used to be the most valuable items. How many of these have changed?
- Why do you think salt or seashells were used as money?

Mystery of the Highlands economy

About 400 years ago there was a major change to the many local economies of the Highlands. This included a big change to the gardening systems, with the introduction of the sweet potato to the area. No one is sure how the sweet potato arrived. Maybe it came through barter. Maybe it was a gift for exchanges.

Quickly different communities in the Highlands developed technologies to grow sweet potatoes using mounds, compost and pigs.

- Some groups in the Southern Highlands have stories of how they experimented with sweet potatoes. First they tried to grow them like yams with vines growing up sticks.
- In Enga there are stories of how they discovered that sweet potatoes would grow in poorer soils and in colder places than taro. Hunting grounds became planting grounds. People experimented and adapted. The biggest mounds are found in Enga. They need to be big to protect the potatoes from the cold.
- Much smaller mounds are found in Eastern Highlands Province where it is not so cold.

The greatest mystery is what the Highlanders were eating before sweet potatoes. People have found stone bowls and tools for grinding. We think that these were for food preparation. Some people think the staple food before sweet potatoes might have been taro. In the Eastern Highlands, a geographer found terraces that were 12 kilometres long. Maybe the people grew taro in these terraces.

How much economic organisation do you think would be needed to make a terrace 12 kilometres long?

The local economy in Papua New Guinea today

We can see that in the past local village economies produced most of what people needed. Over thousands of years people developed very successful agricultural systems. There was no cash economy. Some places did have types of money, but much trade was through barter and exchange. Contact with the rest of the world was limited. The example of the sweet potato shows that people did try new things when they arrived from overseas.

The economy of Papua New Guinea has changed from the past.

1. **Many new technologies are used in the nation to develop and produce resources.**
2. **Trade has expanded and Papua New Guinea trades with many countries in the world.**
3. **Money or cash is now very important.**
4. **People are becoming more specialised in the work they do.**

For you to try

You can find examples of these four changes in your local community.

- Think for a moment about what types of industry or economic activity your community has. Perhaps it is producing rubber or growing taro and yams? Think about how these activities might have changed.
- What types of new technologies are used in your community to develop and produce resources? For example, how many new technologies are there in making a meri blouse with a sewing machine? Or consider gardening technologies used for new plants like corn, pumpkin, choko and sweet potato.
- How many things can you find in your community that are made somewhere else? Can you find examples of overseas products in your community? Are there any products that your community produces to be sold to other countries?
- Finally, how important is money or cash in your community? What happens if you don't have any? How do people survive without money?

Technology

Transportation has developed from foot travel and canoes, although these are still important. Now we also have motor vehicles, roads, commercial shipping and airplanes. People and goods can travel long distances quickly if you have the cash.

New communication technologies give people information from around the country and around the world. This includes the post office, telephones, radios, newspapers, books, magazines, and television in some places.

New types of power are available. There is electricity in cities and towns and in some rural areas. Machines using diesel and petrol now make many types of work easier.

Mining, agriculture, fisheries and forestry all use new technologies.

Manufacturing has grown using new technologies. Papua New Guinea now has a group of factories. These produce manufactured products like soap, biscuits and bottled drinks.

Trade stores across the nation are selling products for cash. There is a new sales system from supermarkets and large stores in the city to some items in village markets. This is part of a new service sector.

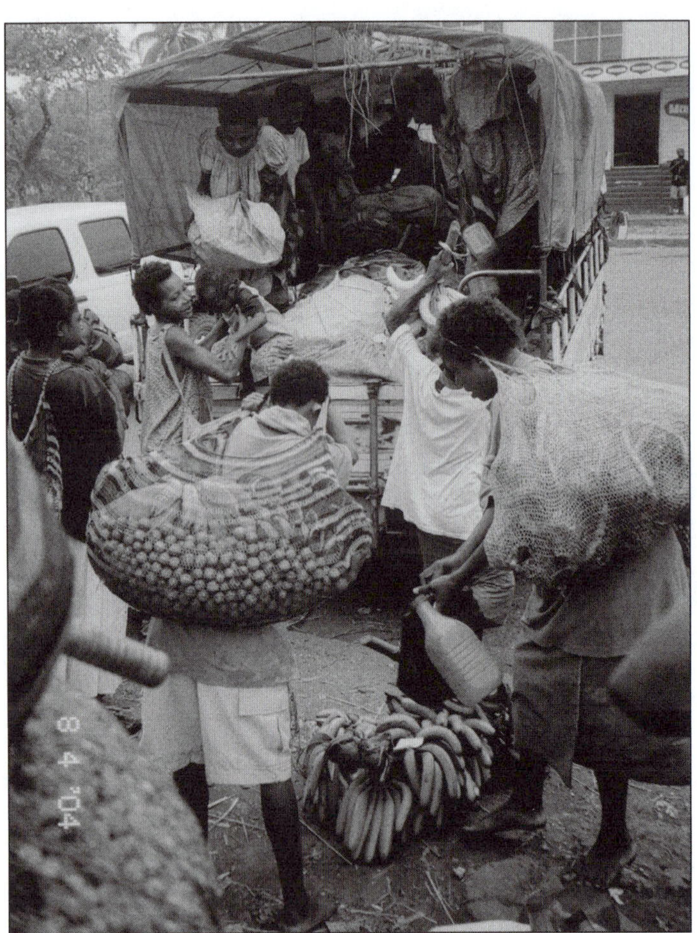

Four parts of an economy

Sometimes a nation's economy is divided into four parts. These are primary, secondary, tertiary and quaternary sectors.

1. The primary sector

Primary industries (or the first industries) make products with little change to them. Gold, coffee, copper and copra production are examples of primary industries. They are often called raw materials.

The primary sector is very important in Papua New Guinea. Much of this sector produces for export. Plantation and cash crops produce coffee, copra, cocoa, tea and spices. Most of this is exported. Forestry and mining are two extractive industries that produce resources for trade. The export of hardwood logs is the major forestry product at present.

Mining means extracting minerals. Traditional mining in Papua New Guinea was for minerals such as clay, obsidian and ochre. Today gold and copper are the two most important minerals mined in the nation. Oil and natural gas are growing in importance as exports.

Another part of the primary sector produces agricultural products for Papua New Guineans to eat. This is another valuable part of the economy. Many people who cannot earn much money rely on garden produce for food. Even people who move to the cities will often practise traditional gardening, either to feed themselves or sell in the market.

Papua New Guinea is one of the few economies in the world where almost everyone has some right to grow food on land. People are often hungry in many other countries because they do not have access to land to grow food. Access to land is a very special part of the economy.

Extractive industries

A gold mine takes the gold out. In the worst cases, the mining company puts nothing back. When all the gold is gone, the mine closes and the community must survive with what is left. This can be a polluted river, mining waste (called spoil) and the empty mine. This can badly damage the local environment and economy.

In the best cases, some of the money that the mine earns is invested in the local community. The best investments are in sustainable work and businesses. This means starting businesses that can continue after the mine closes. A sustainable business will use resources carefully so that they continue to be replaced. Agriculture and tourism are two businesses that can be sustainable. (These businesses can be extractive if they are not done carefully.)

For every 100 people in Papua New Guinea, 85 still rely on garden vegetables grown by themselves or their family. That is the same as saying that 85 per cent of the population still relies on a traditional part of the economy for some of their food.

For you to try

- Invite a speaker from the local council to talk about primary industries in the local community and how these industries meet the needs of the local people. Will these industries meet the need of a growing local population?

2. The secondary sector

The secondary sector changes the primary resources into manufactured items. Goods are made with many changes to them. Manufactured goods like shirts, trucks or footballs are examples. Nearly everyone today in Papua New Guinea has some manufactured item, like a steel axe, a fishhook or a pair of glasses. Most of these come from another country's secondary sector.

Export and import

Export means sending products to other countries for sale. Many of Papua New Guinea's exports go to Australia, Japan, Germany, Korea, China, the United Kingdom, the United States of America, the Philippines, Thailand and Italy.

Import means bringing products to Papua New Guinea for people here to buy. We import PMVs, tinned fish, pencils and radios. Australia, Singapore, Japan, the United States of America, New Zealand, Malaysia, Indonesia, China and Korea have all been important importers to Papua New Guinea.

For you to try

- Look at yourself, your friends and your school. How many secondary sector items can you see? How many are manufactured in Papua New Guinea? Make a list of the items manufactured in PNG and a list of the ones that aren't. How many different countries' products can you find in your community? Make a list of the countries.
- Choose a resource that is near your community if possible, like timber, gold, or copper. Then follow its story from how it is obtained to how it is transformed into other products. Illustrate the process with drawings and pictures.

3. The tertiary sector

The tertiary sector refers to goods and services. Goods are items for sale. They are distributed and sold in the tertiary sector. Look in any trade store and you will see the goods that the store sells. Services are also sold. Having a PMV fixed is a service. The garage that does it is part of the tertiary sector. Hotels and restaurants are part of the tertiary sector, and so is the haus kai.

Industries and their products

All industries produce some type of product for sale.

- For mining, that product might be gold or copper.
- For the tourism industry, the product might be a diving trip in the waters of Milne Bay or staying in a hotel in Madang.
- Making or producing anything can be a type of industry. Think of the bilum industry in Papua New Guinea. Most bilums are made for local use, but some are exported and sold in Australia, Germany and the United States of America.

4. The quaternary sector

The quaternary sector represents the new 'knowledge economy'. It is based on information services. It uses computers and the World Wide Web (www). This allows people to quickly gain information from all over the world. But computer technology is expensive and not available in many parts of Papua New Guinea.

The World Wide Web provides information from around the world. You access the World Wide Web on a computer that is connected to a telephone line. Then you can search the Web for any information you want.

- You can find out what coffee prices are in New York.
- You can find out the latest price for gold.
- You can find maps for any place in the world.
- You can find instructions for growing spices or preserving pig meat.

Some Papua New Guineans use this information now. The World Wide Web is very valuable for people who have it.

For you to try

- Where is the nearest computer to you? Is it connected to the World Wide Web?
- How do you think you could get to use the World Wide Web?
- What information would you look for if you could use the Web?

Formal and informal sectors

There is another way that economists divide the economy. These are the formal and informal sectors. The informal sector is sometimes called the traditional sector or the subsistence sector. It is those parts of the economy that still use the original technologies of Papua New Guinea. The formal sector consists of the new technologies and administration.

The informal economy is just as important as the formal economy. Land and food to eat concern all of us. The subsistence economy is also very important. You may hear or read the term 'subsistence farmer' used to describe village gardeners. It sounds as though these people are just subsisting; that means growing their food and eating it. This is rarely true. Almost all rural people earn some money and participate in the cash economy. In fact, extra garden produce is now often sold for cash.

The division between the formal and informal economy is getting harder to make. A growing population means small industries, markets and roadside markets are all important to the economy. Maybe it is not a true division at all, but just a biased way of describing the economy. What do you think?

The table below provides a guide to economic sectors in Papua New Guinea. Remember, like other parts of the nation's society, changes are happening all the time.

Economic sector	Formal sector	Informal sector
Tertiary	Goods and services	Markets, roadside markets, artefact sales, barter
Secondary sector	Manufacturing	Production of traditional tools and artefacts
Primary sector	Mainly exports — cash crops, minerals	Production of food for home consumption

For you to try

Collect examples of formal and informal economic activities (businesses) in your community. Ask questions and see if you can find out about their good and bad points:

- Do they provide an easy way to have employment or income?
- Are they easy to start?
- Do they provide important goods and services for the community?
- Can men and women participate in them?
- How do they benefit the environment?
- How might they harm the environment?
- What are the most important contributions they make to development in your community?

What is used for money in today's economy?

Today Papua New Guinea uses coins and paper bills for money. These are toea and kina. If you look closely at kina paper bills you can see pictures of traditional types of Papua New Guinea money.

Money is something that everyone in the community recognises and will accept as payment.

For you to try

- Think about your community. How many different ways can you think of that money is used?

The consumer society

To consume means to use something up. The simplest example is food. Everyone consumes food. Similarly, everyone consumes water. So you are a consumer. When people talk about the consumer society, they are talking about people buying things. This is called consumption. Consumers are an important group in communities.

If people buy more and more, their economy may grow. Of course, they will have to work more so they earn the money to buy more. Economies depend very much on consumers in countries like Australia and the United States of America.

There are problems when consumers use too many resources. We can see this problem where people have sold their forests for consumers overseas. There are places in Papua New Guinea where the forests and the money are gone.

In Papua New Guinea at the moment, populations are growing faster than jobs. This limits consumption. Many people in Papua New Guinea cannot consume as much as they want to. They do not have the chance to work as much, or earn as much as they would like.

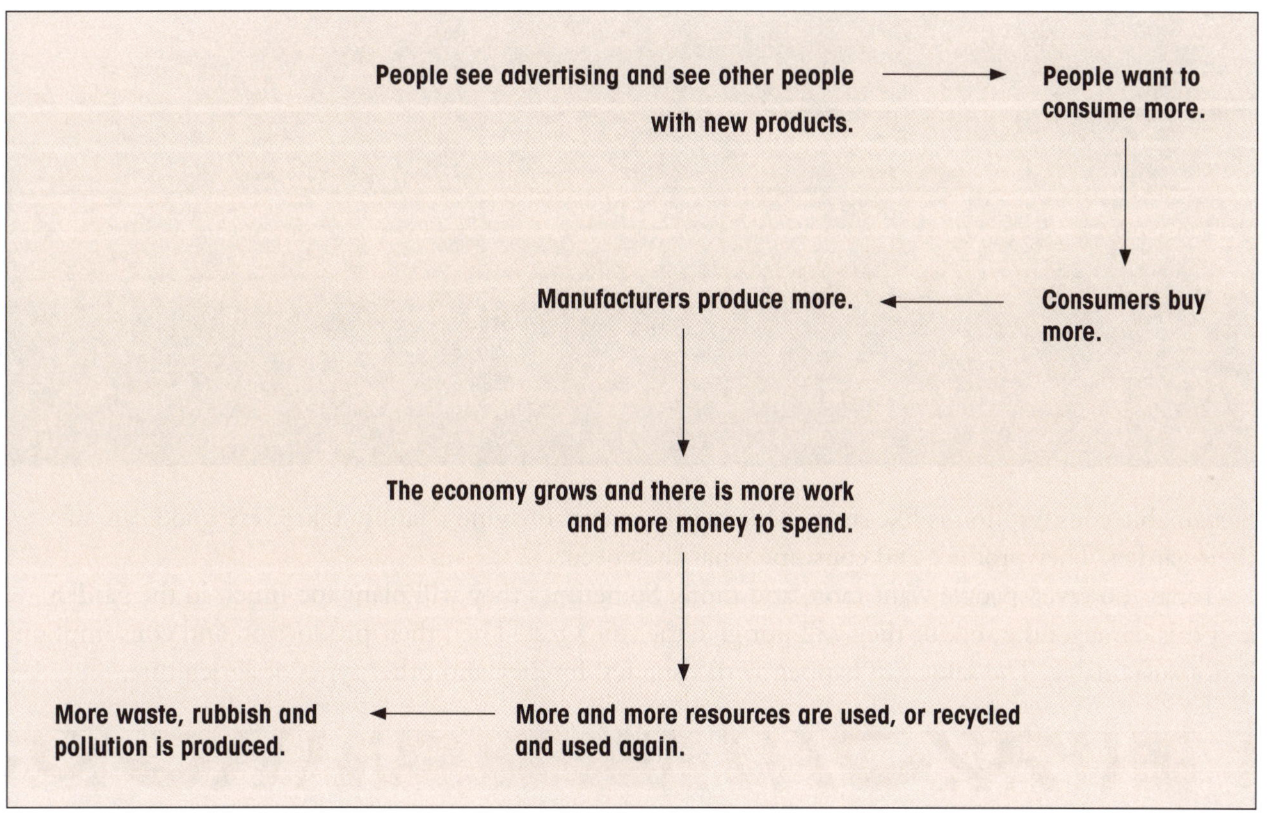

For you to try

- Discuss what type of a consumer you are. Discuss your role as a consumer. What rights and responsibilities does this role have? How can wise consumption contribute to community development?
- Make a table showing the rights and responsibilities of a wise consumer of goods and services.

Sustainable consumption

Sustainable consumption is like sustainable development. Imagine a family takes very good care of their garden. They produce and consume what they need.

Today, however, people want more and more. Sometimes they will plant too much in the garden and this damages the soil, or they will not give the soil a rest. Then their production and consumption is not sustainable. The same can happen with fisheries, forestry and other types of agriculture.

Traditional feasting and other traditional ceremonies can be a time of heavy consumption. It can also be a time to pay back traditional consumer debt. Sometimes people paid in live pigs or pig meat. It was a time when people used their traditional savings. Now, more and more people are changing to cash.

For you to try

There are two extreme types of people in the cash society. One type of person tries to save all the money they get. The other type spends all of it. In between these two types are the rest who spend some and save some.

- Discuss in class, what type of spend-or-save person you are.
- Discuss your attitudes and values about money. Then discuss the attitudes and values for money in your community.
- What type of spend-save situation can you find? Discuss the reasons for this situation.

Community development

Community development can be defined as making things better in the community. They may be economic improvements. Examples of economic development include getting more work or selling resources in the market.

Another way of making the community a better place is to improve education, health, and access to electricity, water, sanitation and transportation. Social development includes improvement to sports, culture and other activities.

Economic assistance for the local community

Many groups want to help local communities with development. These include:

- government departments — help with agriculture or business
- NGOs (non-government organisations) — promote sustainable economic development or appropriate development
- businesses
- international groups — World Bank, Asian Development Bank, AusAID (Australia), JICA (Japan). These groups have programs to provide loans or grants for economic development. A loan you must pay back. A grant is like a gift. You do not have to pay it back.

For you to try

- Invite a local council member to your school to talk about projects or assistance in your community.

Case study: What type of coffee tree should be developed?

Many communities rely on coffee to supply cash income. There have been many development projects to help them. Agriculture researchers have worked to develop the best trees that give the most beans. These trees need good fertilisers and careful pruning each year. Plantations need this type of tree. A plantation needs to produce a lot of coffee each year, so it can pay its workers and make a profit.

But most community coffee growers still follow Melanesian values. They only work as much as they have to or want to, for cash. When coffee prices are high, they pay more attention to their trees. When coffee prices are low, they will not work as much. They do not need high-producing trees. They need a tough tree that can survive long periods with no care.

So what type of tree should be developed to help communities develop?

For you to try

- Look at the cartoon on page 78. Discuss the smallholder and plantation owner's approaches to coffee trees.
- Look for differences in the development needs of the formal and informal parts of your community. Choose an example and write about the differences.

Community development — Problems

Development that requires big changes can be difficult for people. Small changes are easier because they allow people to adapt.

For example, outsiders have tried to introduce rice cultivation to Papua New Guinea for over a hundred years. Smallholders can't use their traditional gardening methods to grow rice. It is a lot of work and does not pay well. Now, some people are growing rice as it becomes more worthwhile economically.

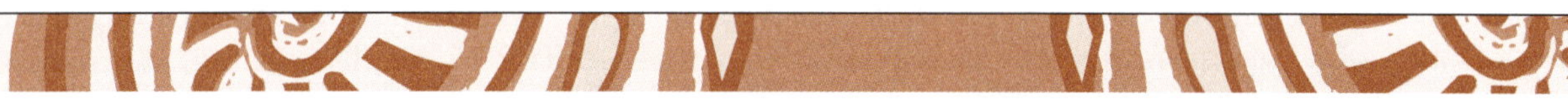

Rural communities are not always grateful for development. Work on Manus Island to provide electricity had to be abandoned because the Electricity Commission could not meet the compensation demands that villages lodged for felled coconut trees along the proposed route. And compensation demands are a fact of life for those involved in infrastructure development in Papua New Guinea (including aid donors), even in instances where the group demanding the compensation is a direct beneficiary of the activity.

From 'The Economy of Papua New Guinea', *International Development Issues*, No. 53, AusAID 2000

For you to try

From the above extract, discuss what a direct beneficiary is. What are direct benefits? Do direct benefits also have costs?

Have class members put on a role play. Some people take the Manus villagers' roles (elders, councillors, landowners, mothers). Other people take the Electricity Commission (Elcom) role. Act out the situation. Have the role players consider:

- Why might people prefer to keep their coconut trees and do without electricity?
- How expensive are electricity bills?
- How good is electric lighting for studying or working at night?
- What are the benefits of electricity, of coconuts, of compensation? What are the costs of these?

Community development — Advantages

Papua New Guineans have been very clever in adapting development to their own local situation. They have been doing this for thousands of years.

For example, Australians owned and managed coffee plantations in the Highlands from the 1950s. Very quickly, Highlanders took coffee seedlings and started growing them in their gardens. They realised this was an opportunity to make cash.

River people grow grass island vanilla

by Beverly Sangamat

Villagers of the Sepik River basin are inventing methods and ideas to beat floods and cultivate grass island vanilla.

The National visited the Sepik last week and saw villagers in Angoram and Ambunti growing vanilla on the grass islands.

Grass islands are large floating patches of areas formed by dead grass, logs and other vegetation deposits found on the lakes and swamps near lowland villages. Small shade trees and vanilla are now being grown on these islands and, in the event of high flood, they can either rise or fall with the movement of the water. These floods have destroyed whole villages. The last high flood experienced was late last year . . .

Meanwhile, the neighbouring villages of Yentchan and Korogu situated on higher grounds have also come up with another system called forking. Here, villagers concentrate on building mounds and pruning their shade trees in a manner in which they can fork out the plant and hang it on these trees if and when there is a flood.

With deteriorating roads and no public river transport reaching their villages from either Wewak or Madang, Korogu people are now calling on vanilla buyers to also go up the river and buy their beans.

Extracted from *The National* 7 Feb 2004

For you to try

- Discuss the article as an example of how people are adapting to their environment and developing a cash crop.

A safe and healthy environment

Good development means providing a safe and healthy environment for the people who live in that community. This type of environment would include:

- access to good food and clean water
- clean air
- housing suited to the environment
- safe places for work, education, recreation, and other activities
- low rates of disease — not many people would be sick (or dying)
- enough resources to support the population
- good transport.

For you to try

- Invite a village elder to explain how people know where the safe drinking water is and where the water is unsafe.
- Look at the two pictures below. List what makes one a safe and healthy place. What makes the other unhealthy and unsafe?

Communities have schools, health centres, police stations, local government and other services. Each of these can help to build a safer and healthier environment.

Schools provide children with important information about the environment. They teach children about the need for clean water and how to protect water supplies. The basic skills of reading, writing and mathematics allow children to understand their environment and how to use it wisely. Traditional education and training also provide people with ways of safeguarding their environment.

Health services help people when they are sick. Many community health officers assist mothers and their children. They may also educate the community on hygiene and sanitation matters. Health officers can explain the dangers of dengue fever and malaria. People can reduce the dangers of these diseases by changing their lifestyle.

The police work to keep the community safe from criminal activity. Many parts of Papua New Guinea still rely on community members to keep the community safe. Many rural communities still follow traditional methods on law and order issues.

For you to try

- Draw a picture or diagram of a safe and healthy environment in your local community. Draw a picture or diagram showing environmental problems in your local community. Discuss your pictures with your parents for their ideas.
- Discuss your pictures in class and see what you can do to help your community achieve a safer and healthier environment.

3

Culture

Chapter summary

In this chapter you will have an opportunity to:

✓ identify and describe the basic features of your local culture/s

✓ discuss similarities and differences in the ways local families celebrate cultural events

✓ identify cultural changes that have occurred in your local culture and express opinions about these changes

✓ describe and participate in local cultural events

Syllabus references

Strand: Culture

Substrand: Cultural Expression

Outcomes

Students are able to:

6.3.1 identify and describe the basic features of local culture and cultures

6.3.2 identify and appraise the changes taking place in local culture

6.3.3 participate in local culture

CULTURE IN OUR COMMUNITIES

Culture is the way of life in a society. We can find culture in all human activity.

- Physically — how people dress, types of houses they have, materials they use
- Socially — how people behave together, values and beliefs they hold

Melanesian culture applies to groups of peoples in Papua New Guinea, Fiji, Indonesian Papua, the Solomon Islands and Vanuatu. Melanesian culture values gift giving and group ownership of land.

The Melanesian culture generally produces new leaders with each generation. The idea of chiefs who are born to rule is more a feature of Polynesian culture. However, chiefs born to rule exist among the Mekeo people of Central Province and the Trobriand Islanders.

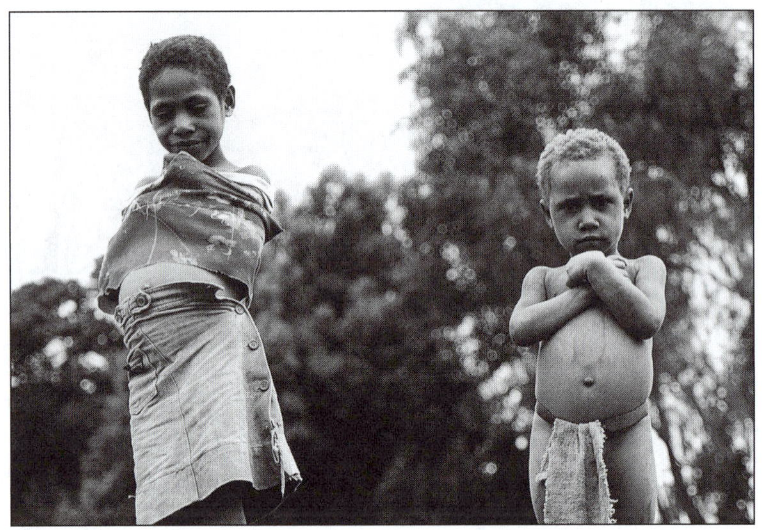

Within Melanesian culture, there are hundreds of other sub-cultures. As well, people have brought ideas, practices and material objects from other cultures to Papua New Guinea. Western and Asian cultures are two major influences on Papua New Guinea.

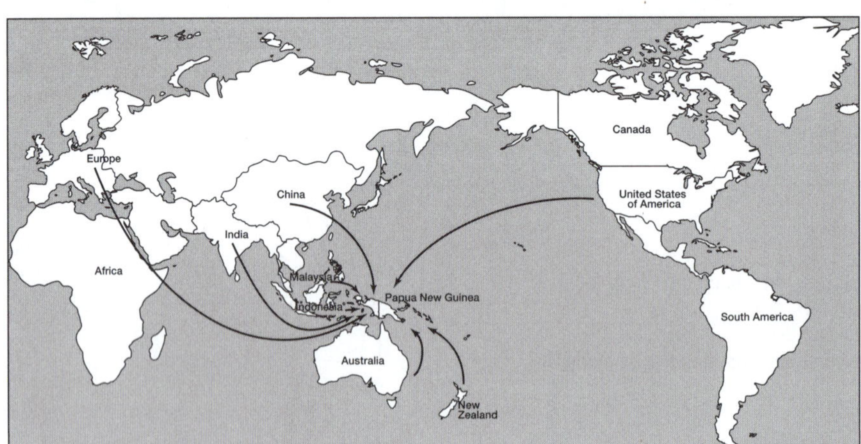

Western cultural influences have come from Australia, New Zealand, Europe and the USA. Asian influences have come from Indonesia, Malaysia, India, China and other parts of Asia.

For you to try

- Look at this picture. How many different cultural influences can you find?

CULTURES ARE ALIVE

Cultures do not stay the same. Cultures change and adapt all the time. There are two ways that cultures change — innovation and appropriation.

1. Innovation is anything new. For example, an innovation can be an invention, new idea, new way of treating relatives or new way of singing a song. The changing styles of pottery in Papua New Guinea are innovations over thousands of years.

The different agricultural systems that we have talked about are innovations. In fact, early Papua New Guineans made great innovations in agriculture. Sugar cane, taro and bananas probably started as crops in Papua New Guinea. Then they were taken to the rest of the world.

2. Appropriation means to take from. Cultural appropriation happens all the time. People take things from other cultures, then use them in their own culture. Cultures all over the world have taken taro, sugar cane and bananas from Papua New Guinea. They have appropriated them from us. We have appropriated many things from other cultures.

Appropriation and innovation often happen together. Something is taken from one culture and used in another culture in a new or different way. This can now happen easily with modern communications, economic systems and transportation. Some people are worried that these rapid changes are leading to a single global culture. This is called globalisation.

For you to try

- What examples of innovation and appropriation can you find in these pictures?
- How many cultures can you identify in your community? What differences do they have? How are they similar?

Cultural expression

Cultural expression is how a culture shows itself. There are many ways of expressing culture such as ceremonies, houses, buildings, food, clothing, land use, transportation and communication. We can also find cultural expression in decoration, art and music. Think about the use of coconut oil or pig grease in Melanesian cultures. Both are important parts of body decoration. This is a type of cultural expression.

Tattoos are a common Melanesian body decoration. The same patterns are sometimes found on pottery. Some tattoos still used by the Motu people are found on pottery pieces hundreds of years old. Innovation changed the decorations on this pottery faster than on people.

Why do you think this happened? One explanation is that the tattoos had more emotional value. You loved your grandmother and she loved her grandmother and you all had the same tattoo. But a grandmother making pottery a long time ago decided on a new design and other people liked it. One part of cultural expression changed. The other did not.

For you to try

- This picture shows cultural expression in body decoration and dress. What do you think the expressions mean to people? Do they indicate any roles?
- Collect pictures or make drawings of dress and body decoration in your community. Label them to explain their meaning and if they indicate any roles.

Special ceremonies

All cultures have special ceremonies for life events. These ceremonies point to different stages in a person's life. These are called RITES OF PASSAGE. We are talking about a person moving (or passing) from one stage to another in life. Four important rites of passage are:

1. birth ceremonies or traditions, where a new member is greeted into the culture
2. ceremonies to become a man or woman and accept adult rights and responsibilities
3. marriage is another point of becoming an adult with more responsibilities and rights
4. death marked by funeral ceremonies and rites to help the living cope with the loss.

Each of these four ceremonies is practised differently in different cultures. Practices are changing all around us in Papua New Guinea. Many places now have a mixture of old and new ways. Look at the table. Then discuss your practices. Are they changing?

Experience	Examples of some traditional practices	Examples of some introduced practices	Your Practices
Birth	Female helper or traditional midwife helps with the birth. Celebrations 30 or 60 days after a successful birth. Special treatment of the umbilical cord, special foods, songs and practices for the newborn child.	Hospital or trained medical staff assist with the birth. Staff monitor and advise mother on infant weight, health, nutrition and hygiene. Newspaper announcement of birth and celebration for each birthday.	?
Becoming a man	Boys leave mother and move to a single men's house. Training by village elders. Circumcision and other ceremonies.	Graduation from school with a graduation ceremony. Special birthday party for reaching 15, 16, 18 or 21 depending on the Western culture.	?
Becoming a woman	Secret women's meetings. Skill training by older women for younger women. Puberty ceremonies.	Graduation from school with a graduation ceremony. Special birthday party for reaching 15, 16, 18 or 21 depending on the Western culture.	?
Marriage	Bride price ceremonies, family meetings, special feasts and exchange of food and gifts. New relationships with in-laws, in some cultures the son-in-law cannot speak to his wife's parents.	The couple has a church or civil wedding that is recorded by the government, followed by a party. The woman may change her last name.	?
Death	Special feasting and community ceremonies; name changing.	A church funeral with the death recorded by the government.	?

For you to try

- Make up a table as for page 88 and fill in practices from your local community.
- Which practices have been introduced and which come from Melanesian culture?
- Look for examples of adaptation, innovation and appropriation in cultural practices.
- Consider people's roles, attitudes and values. Are these changing in ceremonies? How?

Language and culture

Sometimes you will hear people say, 'Papua New Guinea has over 800 languages so it has over 800 cultures.' If a different language is spoken, does it mean it is a different culture?

There is no easy answer. Sometimes a different language does indicate a different culture. But very similar cultures can have different languages. Look at the coast or Highlands of Papua New Guinea. You may hear many different languages but find similar cultures in a local area.

You may also find examples of different cultures that have the same language.

Changes to language

Many new words have been added to languages in Papua New Guinea. Some languages have developed many new expressions. For example, if a bell is ringing, Motu language will say, 'Ia boi boi.' (Does boi boi sound like bell or ringing?)

Politicians now say, 'Mipela laik compromaism' for, 'We'd like to compromise.' Where do you think this idea comes from?

For you to try

- People are innovating with language all the time. Some new words last a long time. Others are called slang and can disappear quickly. What changes can you find in your languages? Are there words for spoon and fork? For computers and holidays? For the number 100 or 1 000?

Religious and spiritual practices

Traditional religions in Papua New Guinea have many different cultural expressions and values. There are many examples of sacred animals, some with special powers. The world is seen to have many spirits. This includes the spirits of the dead who can be dangerous.

Different people have different stories about how human beings began on Earth. Some Melanesian traditions describe how human beings and snakes could both shed their skins. In this way they could live forever. Then the snakes tricked the people. The people could not shed their skins anymore. People could no longer live forever.

Many Papua New Guineans now practise the Christian religion. Places of worship, beliefs and values have changed or been adapted. There are many different varieties of Christian religions. Catholics and Lutherans are the two largest Christian denominations in Papua New Guinea. Other Protestant churches and missionaries still come to PNG.

Some traditional beliefs and practices still remain strong, for example, sorcery. Sometimes Christian and traditional beliefs are mixed as people search for their own cultural meanings.

Art

Art is another example of cultural expression. Art can include carvings and other sculpture, body decoration, painting, singing, music, drama and dancing. Each culture defines what is good art.

Papua New Guinea has a wealth of art and artists. Often Melanesian art is divided into two categories.

- Traditional — as it was done in the past with traditional materials and concepts
- Contemporary — using traditional and introduced materials, concepts and technologies.

Originally most art made in Papua New Guinea was sacred. This means it used religious symbols to strengthen religious beliefs and values. Art is also an important part of many ceremonies. People in the cultural group understand the shared values represented by the symbol. Some symbols may be very simple, like the Christian cross. Others may be complex, like the Malagan figures of New Ireland.

For you to try

- Collect examples of sacred symbols from your community and explain what they mean.

Music and singing

Each region of Papua New Guinea has produced different types of instruments, music and songs. Drums are found in many places. These range from very small hand drums to huge slit gongs. Each area decorates them differently. Flutes vary, from large coastal tubes to the panpipes of the Highlands.

Today you will also find contemporary Melanesian music. There are Papuan New Guinea bands, song groups and choirs. Singing is done traditionally and adapting to many new styles. Some of these groups are religious. Singing is a good way to remember information.

For you to try

- Have different groups and individuals in the class perform their favourite Melanesian music or songs. It can be contemporary, religious or traditional.
- Discuss in class the different purposes of the music and songs.

Singsings

Singsings are an important part of Melanesian culture. There are many different types of singsings and singsing decoration. Collect information about singsings in your community. Make notes and answer these questions:

- What was the purpose of singsings?
- How have they changed?
- Are the decorations still the same?
- Do the same groups of people still hold singsings? Are they still as common as in your grandparents' time?
- Compare the singsings of different cultural groups, if they exist in your community.
- As a class, discuss what is replacing singsings and how this affects your local culture.

Sculpture, other carvings and painting

Papua New Guinea artists are famous around the world for their sculpture and painting. Sculptures are traditionally made from wood. Some places use soft stone. The famous Spanish artist Pablo Picasso was influenced by the art of Papua New Guinea.

The traditional technologies for painting and carving used available materials. Stone axes did heavy cutting. Sharp pieces of shell or obsidian were used for finer carving. An item like stingray skin was used for sanding and polishing. Trobriand Islanders still use squid ink to paint designs onto lime gourds. Many carvings were painted using powdered clay, charcoal, lime and ochres.

Masks, shields, canoe prows, spirit boards, bullroarers, storyboards, ancestor boards and betelnut equipment are all examples of traditional carvings. Today masks and other carvings are made for sale. Sometimes this is called tourist art.

Paintings, prints and drawings are still made by contemporary Papua New Guinea artists. Some of these can be found in museums and private art collections around the world. This part of Papua New Guinea culture continues to influence other cultures.

Painting the human body is an art form found in the Highlands. Other examples of Highlands' visual art include shell-work, baskets, decorative wigs and ornate billums with fur and sometimes even feathers.

For you to try

Look at the different pictures of masks and carvings. Discuss what they mean to you. How are they cultural expressions? What are they telling you about Melanesian culture?

Then interview artists in your local community. Be sure to interview both men and women. Remember, artists can be painters, dancers, singers, musicians, actors, sculptors or carvers. Ask the artists about their experiences and traditions. Use the following questions as a guide.

- How have their traditions changed?
- What are they trying to say with their art?
- What does the decoration mean? Where do they get materials?
- What does the art mean? (Remember, song, dance and drama count too.)
- Who taught them?
- Who will they teach about their type of art?
- What values about art do they think are changing?
- What economic role does their art have?
- What social role does their art have?
- What sacred role does their art have?

Invite an artist to your school to help you create visual art.

- Try making a traditional piece of art from your community.
- Then try making a piece of contemporary art.
- Decorate your classroom with the best pieces.

Changes to cultures

The cultures of Papua New Guinea are changing. Entire languages are disappearing and ways of life are changing.

People still mix old and new ways. For example, Gabi went to the hospital for treatment. The doctor gave him Western medicine. Outside a traditional healer used his hands and mouth on Gabi. He sucked rocks and a little flying fox out of Gabi's body. Gabi had two treatments. He felt much better using both the traditional and introduced systems. The healer was an orderly from the hospital, so he had two roles.

During the colonial times, there were restricted areas in Papua New Guinea. That meant that outsiders could not go in. The idea was to protect local culture and to protect the local people.

Indonesian Papua is the other half of the New Guinea island. The Indonesian authorities there still have some restricted areas to protect local people.

The question is, how long can a community be protected? Do restricted areas actually make communities stronger? Can a government keep people away from the rest of the world? Will people sneak in anyway to take advantage of those being protected?

For you to try

- Do restricted areas help protect cultures? Do they protect local people? Would you like to live in a restricted area? Discuss.

Reasons for change

We can look at the different things that have brought changes to our local communities. These include:

- colonisation
- missionaries
- education
- mass media
- new technologies
- customs and laws
- changing by example
- population growth and migration.

Colonisation

The colonial period in Papua New Guinea did not last for long. First came the Germans and British around 1900. They were quickly replaced by Australia. The Japanese occupied much of Papua New Guinea for a short time in World War Two. After the war the Australians returned for another 30 years, until independence in 1975.

Some Papua New Guineans had very little contact with any of the colonisers. Other communities, like those around Rabaul, Lae and Madang had contact with Germans, Japanese and Australians. Different communities had different experiences and you can explore your own in looking for changes from different colonisers. The colonial times started many changes we still see today.

Tok Pisin reflects the colonial English and German languages. For instance, *maski* comes from the German *macht nichts* which means not important.

For you to try

- Invite an elder to your school to talk about experiences with colonisers.
- See if any changes in your community were caused by the different colonial countries: Britain, Germany, Japan and Australia. Australian colonial rule was the longest in Papua New Guinea. It should be easier for you to find examples of Australian influence in your community.
- You will have to ask people and search hard for some changes.

Missionaries

Missionaries worked closely with the British, German and Australian colonial governments. They brought new ideas of faith and religious practice. These changed many customs. The missionaries also supplied health and education services. (This was in addition to what the colonial government provided.) Missionary schools, aid posts and hospitals are still working today in many rural communities. Some religions have worked to adapt parts of Papua New Guinea culture into religious art. There were also church businesses in colonial times. Some of these are still operating.

Education

Schools have made many changes to the way people think, act and dress. Reading, writing and learning about mathematics are all major cultural changes to Papua New Guinea. The national and provincial governments are trying to have all children start school, and at least finish primary school. New subjects such as Making a Living are being taught. This subject teaches students skills they can apply when they leave school.

Mass media

Mass media is able to communicate with many people. The mass media has been very important in spreading political messages. Books, newspapers, magazines, radio and movies are some examples of mass media that existed in colonial times. However, only a few people were educated and had access to them. Video, television, the World Wide Web and DVDs are other examples of mass media that have come to Papua New Guinea since Independence.

The mass media has made many changes to local culture. One example is the creation of two new groups — the Reds and the Blues, supporters of Australian State of Origin Rugby League.

For you to try

- Make a list of all the types of mass media available in your community. Discuss in class which ones are the most popular. What new roles, attitudes and values can you find in the mass media?
- How does this influence individuals in your community?
- How does it influence different groups in your community?
- How do different groups use the mass media in your community?

New technologies

We have discussed how new technologies have changed culture in earlier chapters. Think how new types of transport, communication and employment have changed parts of the local culture. Here are examples of changes in dress and clothing:

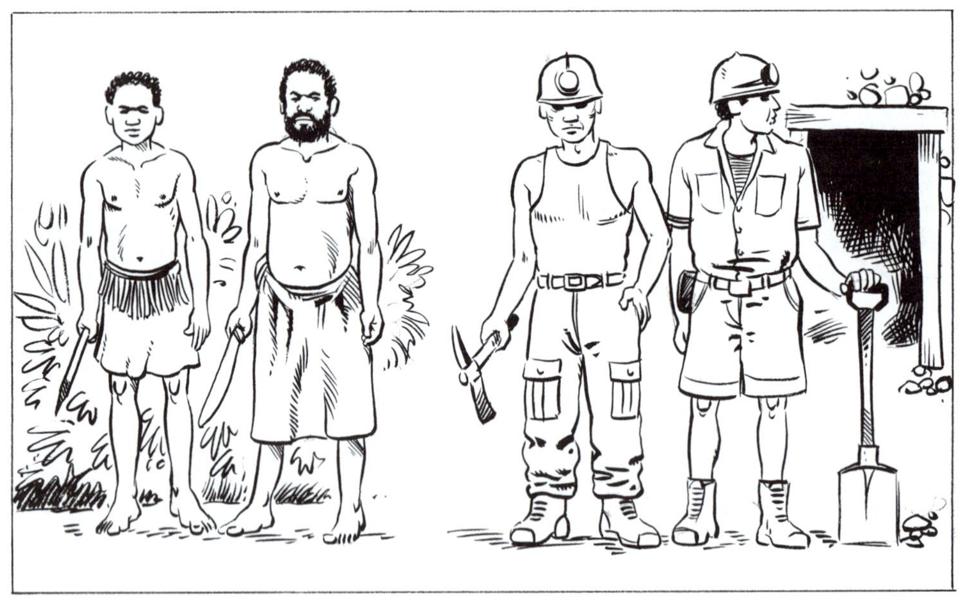

In the colonial period, the authorities often made workers wear lap laps.

Mining and construction industries require workers to wear hard hats, steel-toed boots and protective clothing.

For you to try

- What is the role of clothing?
- Look at the pictures on page 98 and discuss the many changes to dress and clothing in Papua New Guinea. Collect more examples.
- Discuss how clothing is adapted to the environment. Or is it adapted to new cultural ideas?

Customs and laws

Look around you and you will see new customs and changes to old customs. The written legal system of Papua New Guinea is based on the law of Queensland, Australia. But the Papua New Guinea courts also consider traditional values. Some aspects of traditional law still apply.

Changing by example

People can change their culture by copying what people from other cultures do. In Papua New Guinea, colonial workers, tourists and other expatriates have set examples that people followed. Leaders can also influence changes to culture by what they say and how they behave.

People will still copy examples even if it is something they are not supposed to do. Papua New Guineans were not allowed to drink alcohol for much of the colonial period. They watched the colonialists drink beer and other types of alcohol. The example was unhealthy. Drinking a lot of beer or other alcohol is bad. Papua New Guinean males copied this behaviour. At first it was against the law (illegal). Later it became legal when the law was changed. The result is a serious alcohol problem.

For you to try

Discuss in class and at home:

- Has drinking alcohol changed Papua New Guinea culture?
- How have the changes affected women?
- How have the changes affected men?

Population growth, migration and change

The population of Papua New Guinea has been growing fast since Independence. It has grown from around three million people in 1975 to nearly six million people now. This puts pressure on the land and other resources. It can also influence people to migrate.

Human migration is the movement of people from one settlement or place to another. In prehistoric times, several waves of migrating people settled in Papua New Guinea. People continued to move and explore during precolonial times. Today people are able to move more quickly and much further using new transport systems.

Migrants seek new opportunities. There are two major types of migration:

Forced migration is when people have no choice and must move. War is a common cause of forced migration. Some people from Indonesian Papua have come into Papua New Guinea as forced migrants. Natural hazards can force migration — for example, when people had to leave Rabaul because of volcanic eruptions.

Voluntary migration is much more common in Papua New Guinea today. People may choose to migrate because of PUSH or PULL factors. Push factors are things that people do not like about their current place or cause them difficulty. Such features tend to push people out. The situation at home encourages them to migrate. Here are examples of PNG push factors.

- Lack of markets and economic opportunities
- Shortage of land
- Enemies
- Fear of sorcery.

Pull factors are the attractions that draw people to a new place. Here are examples of pull factors.

- Education for children
- Access to computers and the World Wide Web
- Entertainment and recreation (the bright city lights)
- Economic and employment opportunities
- Chance to stay with wantoks (chain migration).

People often find the new place to be more difficult than they thought it would be. Still, many migrants stay once they have moved. They may move in with wantoks at the beginning. This is called chain migration. When they move into their own place, more wantoks may come to stay with them. This continues the chain.

Migration to a new place can be permanent or temporary. Many migrants to towns or cities think they are only moving temporarily and then stay all their lives. Others do go back home. Plantation labour is a common example of temporary migration in Papua New Guinea.

For you to try

- Find a migrant (maybe you are a migrant). Discuss their experience with them. How important were the push and pull factors? Do they think they are temporary or permanent? Write their story and illustrate it.
- Collect the main themes from all the stories. Make a class poster about the migration experiences found in your local communities.

Participating in local culture

Oral culture

The cultures of Papua New Guinea began in oral societies. Oral means spoken. It includes singing, often with special dances. Stories, songs and dances are all good ways to learn and remember things. So oral cultures use song and dance to remember. In these cultures, people need to have very good memories. Older people have special value as keepers of knowledge in oral societies.

For you to try

- Singing and dancing are very important to Papua New Guinea cultures. Use a traditional style to make a new song or dance about knowledge you need for your studies.
- Can you make a maths or health song to help you learn?
- Work in groups or as a class to see if a traditional technique can help you learn and remember more.

Time of darkness

Information was passed down through the generations. Very important events were kept alive as stories. One good example of this is the 'time of darkness' story that is told in parts of the Highlands. The time of darkness is when the sky becomes like night. Crops die and people must stay inside their houses for three or four days or they can die.

The story is a warning about what to do when a major volcanic explosion releases material for hundreds of kilometres into the Highlands. The air is filled with fine volcanic dust. This dust can injure lungs and harm people's health. It damages and kills crops. The last such major event happened hundreds of years ago, but the story is still being told. This is one way people passed on knowledge about a natural hazard.

For you to try

- Collect traditional stories and ceremonies from parents, grandparents and other older people. Share them with the class and discuss what you can learn from them. Discuss where the stories can be kept so they are safe for future Papua New Guineans.

Protecting the environment

The people in the village of Kandrian, Pililo Island, West New Britain Province, have a traditional ceremonial mask or a Tumbuan called 'Kamutmut'. The 'Kamutmut' has the power to restrict the whole community from doing certain things. During traditional ceremonies the 'Kamutmut' appears among the people, It is dressed in banana leaves and flowering plants. On its head is a painted mask which has eyes, ears and a pointed face.

The 'Kamutmut' protects the environment by placing restrictions on a certain fishing ground. The whole community and/or visitors are totally forbidden from entering that particular area. Special permission must be obtained from the 'Warkulolo' (the person who represents the mask) before permission is granted to enter that area. Offenders are punished by having to pay compensation in the form of pigs, cash and traditional shell money. This restriction ensures that the area is protected from over-fishing and not used during the fish breeding season.

Restrictions may also be placed for economic reasons. People may be prevented or restricted from getting green coconuts from the coconut trees. This means there will then be enough dried nuts for making copra.

Drama

Acting out stories is a type of drama. Some villages have groups who act out stories. Some of them are very funny stories to make people laugh. There are groups of professional Papua New Guinea actors who perform in theatre. Often the performances are given outdoors. Examples include the National Theatre Company of Papua New Guinea, the Raun Raun Theatre based in Goroka, and the Dua Dua theatre.

Some groups use drama as role play. This is a good way to communicate to people. It can help people understand about problems. Some non-government organisations (NGOs) have used drama to tell about HIV/AIDS.

For you to try

- If safe, perhaps your class can enter a local cultural event. (Independence celebrations may provide the class with an opportunity to sing, dance, tell a story or act out a drama.)
- Watch and study a cultural event to explore how it is organised and if it is successful. Then discuss what might happen to it in the future. Do you think it will stay the same or do you think it will change? Be sure to explore the different roles of males and females. Write down how you think they might be changing now and in the future.

We have looked at important cultural events like funerals and marriages. Now consider some other events. Make a table of these cultural events that you have been in. How many had some traditional element of food, dress, language, dance, song, story, art or some other item? How many are new to Papua New Guinea? (Hint, see the table below for examples of cultural events.)

Cultural event	**Traditional part**	**New part**	**Changes in future**
Birthdays			
Feasts			
Dances			
Plays			
Movies			
Drama			
Sporting events			
Political rallies			
Others you think of			

Integrating Projects

Chapter summary

In this chapter you will have an opportunity to:

✓ learn and use the social science process

✓ using a variety of sources identify the needs of the local community

✓ learn how the local community contributes to provincial development

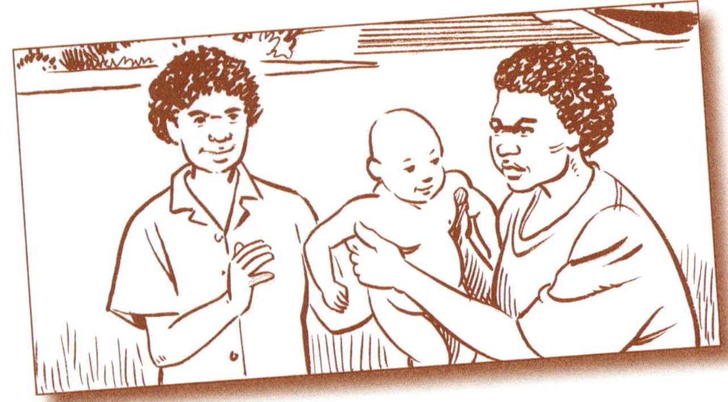

Syllabus references

Strand: Integrating Projects

Substrand: Societies and Communities

Outcomes

Students are able to:

6.4.1 improve the life of the community by gathering and evaluating information about it and taking appropriate action

6.4.2 identify and describe how local communities contribute to the life of their province

STUDYING YOUR COMMUNITY

We have looked at communities in many different ways. You can see that there are many questions we can ask about a community. For example:

- What do people in a community eat?
- What type of problems do people have?
- What type of games do they play?
- What makes them happy?
- Why are they fighting?
- What type of families do they have?
- What is their past?
- What jobs and industries are they in?
- How do they interact with the environment and what are their resources?

The social science process

We can study groups, people and our community using social science. We have a process or a way to do this. We call it the social science process.

The social science process starts with observation. This means looking and hearing. You can form an idea or ask a question from what you see and hear. Many scientists call this a hypothesis. The social scientist takes the idea and starts to study it. Here is an outline of how it works.

Observation

You see and or hear something in your community. This leads you to ask a question or have an idea about it.

Idea or question or hypothesis (an idea to be studied)

You as a social scientist think about what is happening in a group or community.
You might consider different areas, for example, economic, social, geographic or gender.

Gathering information

Next, you gather all the information you can. For example:

- Observing your community
- Observing groups and actions
- Talking to people
- Carefully recording information
- Using books, radio and other sources

Evaluating the information

You can combine the different answers or compare different results.

Making conclusions

- Is the idea right or wrong?
- Can we predict what will happen in the future by using this idea?
- Maybe it is partly correct.
- What can now be done?
- Maybe some action can be taken.

We can conclude that people come to the market for two reasons. One is to talk to each other. They learn the local news and meet friends. The other is to make some money.

Repeating the study

Someone else should be able to go to the same market and form a similar answer or show how attitudes have changed over time.

Gathering and evaluating information

Social science collects or gathers information. There are many ways to do this. Here are some examples:

- Talking to people and asking them questions
- Watching what people do
- Listening to what people say
- Studying records, reports and books
- Asking people to fill in questionnaires
- Working with people to understand their lives

Different ways of collecting information are used in different communities. For example, if people cannot read or write, asking them to fill in a questionnaire is not a good idea.

It is also important to collect information that covers the whole problem. For example, what if you wanted to find out why Grade Six students have problems studying. If you only asked students in Grade Six you would only get part of the answer. You would need to ask teachers and parents as well. You would also need to see what work on this problem had already been done. This would give you ideas for questions that you could ask students, teachers, parents and education staff.

It is also important to collect information from many people. Your information would not be very good if you only asked your friends and the teacher you most like. It is important to have a study that covers different types of people. Then you can be sure that your work is good.

Evaluation

Evaluation comes after you have collected information. Evaluation means thinking about the information you have collected. It means examining the information. This is like the teacher examining your knowledge on a subject.

It is good to talk with others about the information you have collected. You can discuss it with your teacher and fellow students. Sometimes this will lead to further questions. For example, what if you found that students had problems studying at night because of bad lighting? Does this mean that the real problem is people not having enough money to afford lighting? Or the problem may be that the community does not have electric power at night. Or parents may think light is not important for study.

Many times, one question will lead to another. It is often easy to find an answer when you discover what the problem is. Wait and listen before you give your answer to a community problem. It is wise to listen to possible answers given by the community members. Then you can work with them to help solve a problem.

An example from science

Social science is similar to science. Here is an example of how science works.

The scientists in this example are dentists at the University of Papua New Guinea. Dentists look after people's teeth. The dentists saw some people with bad teeth. The dentists' idea was that chewing betel nut was bad for teeth. They looked at many people who chewed betel nut and examined their teeth. They watched people chew betel nut and again examined their teeth. The information that the dentists collected showed that people used their teeth to open up the betel nuts. This actually helped to clean the teeth.

The dentists found that betel nut was not bad for teeth. This surprised them. They admitted that their idea was wrong. This is the power of science. Every idea is tested. Each time we learn something new.

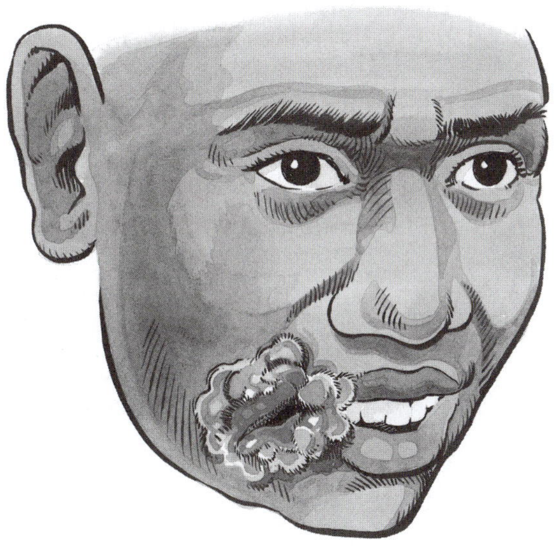

Does this mean that chewing betel nut is good for you? The dentists found no problem with the betel nuts, but other scientists have. They found that it is the lime chewed with the betel nut that can cause cancer of the mouth. People who put the lime on the same spot for a long time have a higher chance of mouth cancer.

Still this does not really answer the question, 'Is chewing betel nut good for you?'

Some experts might tell you that chewing betel nut in a group of people helps people become better friends. Historians might find records that show how important betel nut has been in some Papua New Guinea societies. Others might tell you that betel nut production is an important part of the Papua New Guinea economy. Betel nut is providing wealth to some coastal communities and to market traders in many communities.

As a social scientist, you can see that there are many ways of looking at an idea. Best of all, these things are happening right around you. All you have to do is start thinking about them. Discuss them. Gather information and examine the results.

For you to try

Choose a question or idea for your own research. Keep your study simple. Your teacher will help you choose a topic. Follow the steps for social research. Write down what you have done and the results. Check each step of the process with your teacher.

1. Identify the problem or need in the community. You could use a problem at your school for example.
2. Decide on questions.
3. Select ways of gathering information.
4. Collect information.
5. Analyse and evaluate the information.
6. Suggest solutions.
7. See if the solutions work.

CONNECTIONS BETWEEN THE PROVINCE AND ITS COMMUNITIES

Papua New Guinea has 19 provinces and the National Capital District. Provinces provide a level of government and provide services to different communities and districts. They are part of the governing system that has grown with Independence. The New Organic Law of 1995 made changes to provinces. The Provincial Governor is now the member for the National Parliament.

If you study a map of Papua New Guinea you can see that the provinces have different types of boundaries. The rivers, the sea and mountains make some of the boundaries. Look at your own provincial boundaries. Can you explain what communities and people they include?

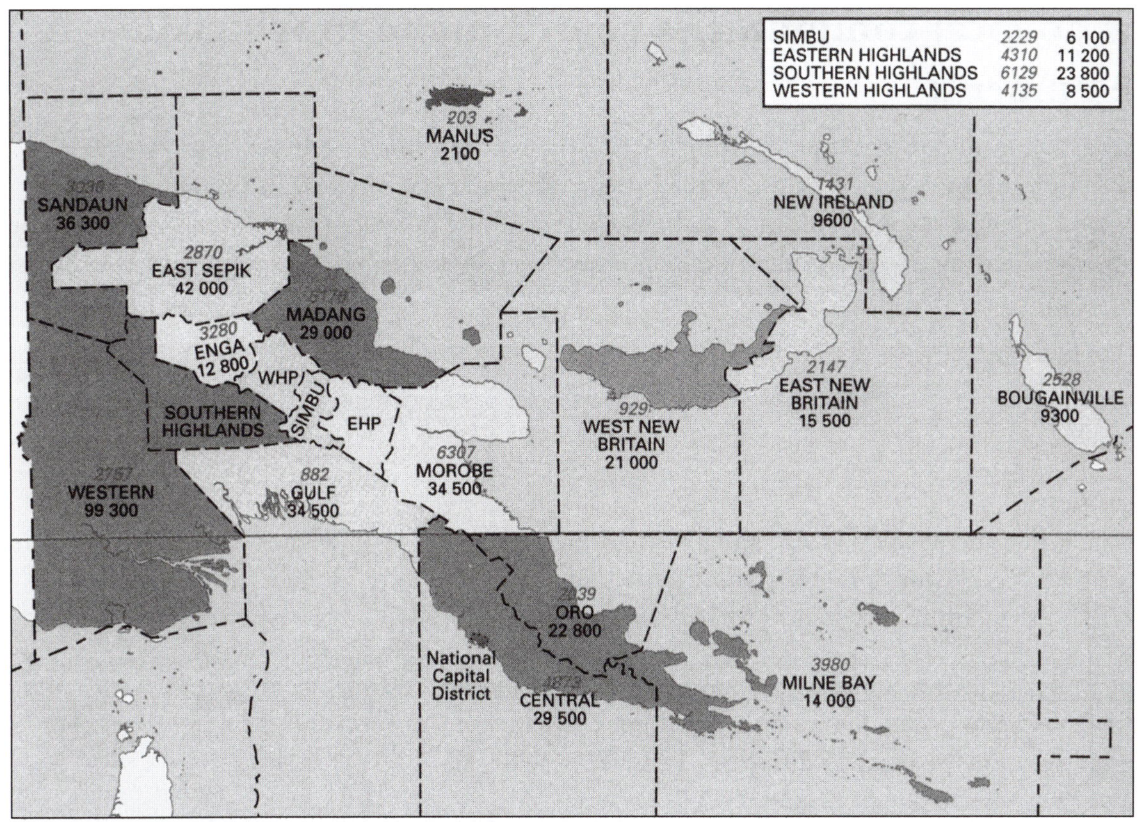

Papua New Guinea has 19 provinces and the National Capital District.

Provincial government is responsible for parts of:

- Education
- Health
- Law and order
- Business, resource and agricultural development
- Other services

How do local communities contribute to provincial development?

It is important to understand that different communities contribute in different ways to the province. Communities that are close to the provincial capital can often contribute more than isolated communities. Communication and transportation for isolated communities may limit their participation. Here are four ways that local communities may contribute to the life of the province:

- Government
- Population
- Economy
- Culture and social

Government

Provincial governments are part of Papua New Guinea's democracy. The voters elect the government members. All eligible voters in every community are allowed to vote. Voting is at the heart of democracy. Each community helps provincial governments and democracy when their people vote.

Papua New Guinean communities have adapted Melanesian customs to democracy. Groups and clans often battle for votes. Candidates sometimes provide gifts of food and drink to voters. Sometimes people even try to vote twice at different places. This is illegal.

Population

The national government provides some funds to the provincial government for services to the people. The level of funding is based on the number of people living in a province. The population of each community contributes to the total population of the province. There are often arguments over the funding.

Economy

Larger businesses in communities pay taxes and charges to the national government. Some of this money should come back to the provinces via funding to the provincial government. Some communities have very large resource projects and these should contribute taxes and royalties to the national government.

Cultural and social

The different social and cultural traditions of communities help define the culture of the province. The idea of having provinces is relatively new. Many of the traditions in the communities are very old so communities are helping to blend the old with the new.

For you to try

- Discuss in class how your community is part of the province. How does your community help the province?

Glossary

adapt	to take something and change it for your needs
animals	includes all living creatures. Examples are insects, fish, wallabies and bacteria
association	a type of social organisation that is not very formal. Examples: A sports club is an association. A rascal gang is an association
attitudes	the way you feel about something. Examples: what you like or do not like
bias	liking something unfairly. Making a judgement to suit oneself or one's group. Similar to prejudice
carving	a wood object, cut by hand, to represent something.
climate	type of weather a place may have for many years. Examples are warm and tropical along the coast, cooler in the mountains
community	a local group. Examples: Villages are communities. Gerehu suburb in Port Moresby is a community
community development	making things better in a community
ceremonies	special times with special activities. Examples: Birthdays and funerals
culture	way of life for a society. We can find culture in all human activity
development	making things better
diet	the food that a person or animal eats regularly. People have many different diets
economy	how people use and distribute resources
environment	everything around us. Urban environments are everything around you in the city. Rural environments are everything around you in the countryside
fauna	another word for animals
fertilisers	natural or manufactured chemicals to help plants grow (include animal droppings and compost)
flora	another word for plants
geology	a science that studies Earth's crust, what is under the ground; road cuttings are a good place to see your local geology

group	more than one. A group of people can be two or more people
institution	a type of social organisation that is formal. Examples: A hospital is an institution. The army is an institution
kinship	people related by blood or marriage
landforms	natural features on Earth's surface. Examples are hills, valleys, rivers and beaches
landscapes	how the land looks. Examples are mountain, forest, urban landscapes. An urban landscape is how the city looks
map	representation of all or part of Earth's surface. Maps can help us to explore parts of our environment
mass media	organisations that communicate with many people. Examples are newspapers, comic books, books, radio, television and the World Wide Web
money	something that everyone thinks is valuable and will accept for payment.
natural resources	something of value from nature like timber, gold, oil and gas
pesticides	chemicals to kill insects
prejudice	judging without knowledge and having an opinion based on ignorance. Similar to bias
population	total number of people in a place. The PNG population is over five million
resource	something of value. Examples: You are a resource. Gold is a resource. An education system is a resource.
responsibilities	duties, things you must do
rights	what you are entitled to have. A clan member will have a right to some clan land to use
role	what a person is supposed to do in a social position. Examples: The role of a leader is to guide the community. The role of police is to keep law and order.
sanitation	cleanliness. It can also mean human waste. A sanitation system takes away human waste (pek pek).
sculpture	made from stone, like a carving
social organisation	how people organise themselves. A family is one type of social organisation. A school is another type of social organisation
soil	ground, thin surface layer that covers Earth's crust. Examples are sandy, loam or volcanic material
solid waste	rubbish
sustainable	something that can keep going for a long time
tourists	visitors who come to a place for a short time. They may be from another part of the country or they may be from overseas
values	beliefs that do not change quickly. Example: Saying, 'A good person helps a wantok' expresses a value
vegetation	plants. Examples are kunai grass, seaweed, forests and swamp plants like sago palms

Project Ideas

Look at the physical environment of your school. Propose ideas to improve the physical environment. Collect ideas from others on how to improve the physical environment of the school. See if you can find one idea that staff and students agree on. Get staff permission to put your idea into practice.

Do a study on the natural hazards of your community. Determine what is the most common natural hazard. Present your report to community leaders. Ask community leaders about what is being done to prepare for this hazard.

Find a place where forest meets the grassland. Dig small holes to see the difference between grassland soil and forest soil. Go further into the forest and see if the soil changes again. Do the same in the grassland away from the forest. BE SURE TO FILL IN THE HOLES AFTER YOU HAVE DUG THEM AND STUDIED THEM. Discuss your findings. What reasons are there for any differences?

Look for erosion in your community. Study how much erosion is made by human activity. How much is natural? Write up your best examples. Make models of cases you find.

Make a model or poster of how your community has adapted to the natural environment.

Do a study of how diets have changed in your community. Find out what people used to eat and what was taboo. What was scarce? Compare the past diet to the present one. Consider how you could improve your diet.

Find a social scientist. Look for an anthropologist, geographer, or some other social scientist. Many development projects will have a social scientist. See what type of research the scientist is doing. See if there is an opportunity for you to participate.

Do a class study about people's attitudes to markets and shops. Find out what people prefer. Compare different group attitudes. Who likes shops? Who likes markets? Who likes both?

Make an association. Discuss what different associations do in your community. Decide on an association your class could make. Have people elected to different roles in the association. Make up a set of rules for the association. See if you can keep it going for a month.

Have a barter market at school. Bring things you want to trade. Barter only; do not use any money.

Discuss in class how well a barter market works.

Develop a set of taboos to stop pollution. Try to practise them. Will it improve your environment?

Role play a special ceremony. Have different class members work on different parts of the ceremony. See how many different types of cultural expression you can include.

Invite a carver, singer, sculptor or other artist to class. Have this person teach you about basic skills. Try to copy or create their type of art.

Collect examples of mass media. Try producing an example for the school. It could be a magazine, book, newspaper or some other form of mass media.

Write and perform a play. It could be about development. It could be about protecting the environment. It could be about attitudes, values, prejudice and bias. It could be about Melanesian culture and how it is changing. You could perform songs and singsings instead of a play.

START
1
2
3
Listened carefully to people's problems
Move 4 points forward
4
5
6
7
8
39
Started community meetings to improve sanitation
Move 3 points forward
40
41
42
43
Did not listen to other people's ideas
Move 3 points backward
44
Fishing Royalty
66
Shared fishing royalties with all village families
Move 4 points forward
65
64
38
37
63
Sold all the village forest
Move 6 points backward
62
61
60
36
35
Stole a pig and shared it with wantoks
Move 6 points backward
34
33
32
31
Mixed traditional and modern values to damage the environment — killed five birds of paradise
Move 3 points backward

stones
ranger
points
ward
10
11
12
Wrote down three ancestor stories from old people to keep for family
Move 5 points forward
13
14
15
16
Used grandparents' knowledge to collect natural foods
Move 3 points forward
46
47
Helped friend understand values
Move 6 points forward
48
49
50
51
Consumed alcohol and started fighting
Move 5 points backward
17
18
52
19
68
69
FINISH
REACH YOUR HOUSE AND LAND
53
20
Told a prejudiced joke
Move 3 points backward
54
59
Showed children how to build a shelter adapted to the environment
Move 2 points forward
55
Sold all my ancestor artefacts, so nothing left for children
Move 3 points backward
21
58
57
56
22
27
Mixed traditional and modern values to stop a tribal fight
Move 6 points forward
23
Slept under a treated mosquito net
Move 3 points forward
29
28
26
25
24

Acknowledgments

The author and publisher wish to thank the following copyright holders for granting permission to reproduce the following illustrative and textual material:

Torsten Blackwood/Newspix, pp. 30, 107; Crawford House Publishing, pp. 13, 14 (bottom centre), 18 (bottom), 21, 63, 71, courtesy of Crawford House Publishing; Phil Korare, p. 105; Chris Mellor/ Lonely Planet Images, pp. 16 (left), 113 (top); Oxford University Press UK, pp. 34 (top and bottom), 116; Alex Steffe/Lochman Transparencies, pp. 18 (centre), 19 (top), 81 (left); *The National*, PNG, 'Villagers threaten to close airport', *The National*, 5/1/04, 'River people grow grass island vanilla' by Beverly Sangamat, *The National*, 7/2/04; Angela Wylie/Fairfax Photos, p. 16 (top right).

Additional photographs supplied by Stephen Ranck and Irene Sawczak.

Every effort has been made to trace the original source of copyright material contained in this book. The publisher would be please to hear from copyright holders to rectify any errors or omissions.